DICTIONARY OF
FLORISTRY
AND
FLOWER
ARRANGING

DICTIONARY OF
FLORISTRY
AND
FLOWER
ARRANGING

Anthony Gatrell

Illustrations by the author

B T Batsford Limited London

For Peter and Anthony

© Anthony Gatrell 1988
First published 1988

Typeset by Tek-Art Ltd, Kent
and printed in Great Britain by
The Bath Press, Bath
for the publishers B T Batsford Ltd
4 Fitzhardinge Street, London W1H 0AH

British Library Cataloguing in Publication Data

Gatrell, Anthony
   Dictionary of floristry and flower
   arranging. — (Batsford vocational
   handbooks)
   1. Flower arrangement
   I. Title
   745.92

ISBN 0-7134-5904-2

Introduction

In compiling this *Dictionary of Floristry and Flower Arranging* (worded in that sequence only because it sounds more in harmony) I am conscious that there are those who believe the former follows a professional career and the latter pursues a vocation, notwithstanding the fact that much flower arranging is undertaken for a fee. The florist is in business to be profitable and uses cut flowers and foliage grown for the mass market, whereas the flower arranger considers the primary source of inspiration to be the garden, plant material from which is supplemented, if necessary, by florist's flowers. All the same, the differences can be exaggerated. Many of the skills and techniques are shared, and the knowledge required to undertake either activity is common to both.

Currently there are many books available on the subject of Flower Arranging, and several books on Floristry have also been published recently. Some have included a brief glossary, but there is no single volume which explains all the terms likely to be encountered in the study of Floristry or Flower Arranging Courses. This is especially true of terms which derive from the related disciplines of Botany and Horticulture and from the study of Gardens, and which have to be gleaned from many different sources.

The idea for such a *Dictionary* came while I was studying for a City and Guilds 730 FETC Course and contemplating an exercise in which I was asked to specify a syllabus for a Flower Arranging Course. Discussing 'vocabulary', I realised that a reference book for the technical terms did not exist. From that particular flash of inspiration – 'Insight' – the idea was conceived. Two years later it has become a reality.

This *Dictionary* therefore includes explanations for all the various words and terms that are in wide usage in Floristry and Flower Arranging. It will assist student and teacher alike in their common understanding and revision work. Many important areas are covered in detail, especially where colour and design are concerned.

Inevitably I have included many botanical terms, but these have been confined to aspects of physical structure and methods of reproduction, in order to cover the general requirements for the City and Guilds Floristry and Flower Arranging (Creative Studies) Courses. Several very good dictionaries for Botany are available if more detailed information is needed.

I have had wide experience of organising Horticultural Shows in a village along with the attendant complexity of producing schedules for Floral Art classes.

I have also exhibited in such Shows and been a judge at others and have

3

drawn upon my experience as a student of Parts I & II 784 C and G Flower Arranging and Part I 019 C and G Floristry Courses. I have illustrated the *Dictionary* with my own simple line drawings, in order to explain some entries more clearly.

This *Dictionary* thus aims to reinforce the understanding of skills and techniques, leaving readers scope to exercise their imagination and creativity in the development and enjoyment of their designs. I hope that it will serve this purpose.

Acknowledgment

I wish to thank the JD and SE Committee of NAFAS for permission to quote from the NAFAS *Judges' Manual and Schedule of Definitions* and in particular Elspeth Haller for her assistance. I am also grateful to the Society of Floristry Ltd, for permission to quote from the *Definition of Terms used in Floristry*, March 1987 edition.

I am indebted to the tutors of the Courses which I have attended who all encouraged me and opened my eyes to the art forms of floristry and flower arranging: Mavis Brooker, Mike Burgess, Maureen Ockenden and especially Janette McKeown to whom I owe so much for giving me the opportunity to develop my interest in the subject both during the Part II 784 Course and since.

Rona and Stanley Coleman helped me in many other ways, notably by suggesting modifications to certain entries and by providing source material for many Floristry illustrations. I am most grateful to them for their kind enthusiasm and encouragement.

Janet Smith read the manuscript and has made some most useful comments to several entries and I acknowledge her kindness and also welcome the association we have on the NAFAS Teachers' Association Editorial Board.

Peter Gatrell made significant improvements to the style of the entries.

My debt also extends to Coppelia Tatley who produced the typescript with great care and interest, as a result of which she may yet be persuaded to channel her artistic flair towards flower arranging. Thelma Nye, a Senior Editor at Batsford, has encouraged me from the outset and shown constant interest in the project.

My initial interest in Flower Arranging developed from being married to a superb flower arranger. Without Mary's interest I doubt if mine would have 'flowered'. She has given me invaluable support throughout and I owe her more than I can say.

The dedication is to reciprocate those given to their mother and father by our twin sons, Peter and Anthony, in their respective academic books. They will know that it gives me so much pleasure to dedicate this work to them and their dear families in turn.

Chedworth 1988

AWG

Abbreviations

L = Linnaeus
l.s. = longitudinal section
t.s. = transverse section
Opt. app. = optical appearance
Psycho. eff. = psychological effect
Symb. interp. = symbolic interpretation
DNA = Deoxyribonucleic acid
RNA = Ribonucleic acid
NT = National Trust
∞ = numerous or infinite
var. = variety

A

A
The symbol for the number of stamens in the floral formulae, eg Primulaceae = K(5) C(5) A5 G̲(5) thus A5 = 5 stamens.
See also *Floral formula* and *Androecium*

Abaxial
The underside of a leaf, pointing away from the stem. See also *Adaxial*

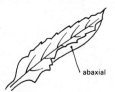

abaxial

Abscisic acid
A naturally occurring plant hormone that promotes leaf fall and which also inhibits root growth and germination. See also *Abscission*

Abscission
The natural separation of a leaf or stalk from a stem of a plant, controlled by abscisic acid. An abscission layer forms at the base of the leaf stalk

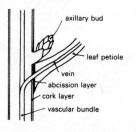

axillary bud
leaf petiole
vein
abcission layer
cork layer
vascular bundle

(petiole); it eventually disintegrates completely so that the leaf falls.

Absorption
The movement of fluid across a cell membrane, eg plants absorb water and mineral salts from the soil through their roots; also chlorophyll in leaves absorbs and stores energy from sunlight (photosynthesis).

Abstract
A design concept using plant material in a non-naturalistic manner. The unification and organization of all the elements are restricted to the simplest forms, with an emphasis on space, visual movement and creativity.
See also *Expressive Abstract* and *Decorative Abstract*

Acanthaceae   K(4-5) C(4-5) A4 G̲(2)
Small family of Acanthus of which mollis and spinosus are the species best known to flower arrangers.

Accent
The distinctive characteristic of an exhibit; to give special emphasis to an aspect of a design by employing colour, form, contrast, etc, thereby drawing attention to the particular feature or contrasting detail.

Accessories
Any objects *other than plant material*

7

which are added to an exhibit to give additional character and/or to enhance the theme portrayed, and which may be obligatory in a show schedule.

NB Accessories which may be decorated in any way, do *not* include manufactured replicas of flowers, foliage and fruit in any material as these are considered *artificial plant material*, the use of which is only permitted as stated in show schedules.

See also *Artificial plant material, Backgrounds, Bases, Containers, Drapes, Made-up plant material* and *Title cards*

Accessories (in floristry)
(1) Suitable objects used in conjunction with a design to emphasize the theme, eg 'Stork' for a christening arrangement.
(2) Accessories such as a hat, handbag, prayer-book carried or worn at a wedding or similar occasion to which a suitable corsage is attached.

Accidental colour
See *After-image*

Accidental light
Any form of light that is not daylight such as candle-light, moonlight or fire-light.

Acclimatization
See *Harden-off*

Aceraceae K4-5 C4-5 or o A8 $\underline{G}$(2)
Very large family of trees and shrubs (*c* 200-300 species). All but two species are the Maples within the genus Acer.

Achene
A small, hard, dry indehiscent fruit

formed from a single carpel and containing one seed.
See also *Indehiscent, Nut* and *Samara*

Achromatic colour
Free from colour, or devoid of chroma, ie any gradation of white, grey or black which has a neutralising effect on other colours. Also referred to as *Neutral colours*.

Acicular
A leaf shape that is needle or awl-like.

Acid soil
A soil with a pH of less than pH7 (which is neutral). Most acid soils are from pH4.6-5.5 and are prevalent in districts of high rainfall and sandier soil. The natural vegetation supported on acid soils is heath, heathers, bilberry, gorse and conifers.

Actinomorphic
Types of flower structure which when cut horizontally as a transverse section, display radial symmetry. If cut vertically in two they are also symmetrical. See also *Zygomorphic*

Acuminate
A leaf apex ending in a long point.

Abruptly acuminate – round or blunt towards the end then suddenly drawn out to a fine point.

Long acuminate – uniformly acuminate from well down the leaf.

Short acuminate – acuminate for only a short distance from the tip.

acuminate

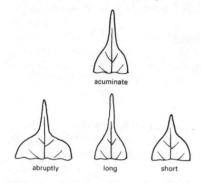

abruptly   long   short

Acute
A leaf apex ending in a sharp angle.

Adaxial
The upper side of the leaf, pointing towards the stem. See also *Abaxial*

adaxial

Adjacent complementary colours
A contrasting harmony of three hues, namely one hue, its direct complement, along with *either* of the adjacent complementary hues, eg

(a) Blue:orange and Yellow/orange
or Blue:orange and Red/orange

(b) Red:green and Yellow/green
or Red:green and Blue/green

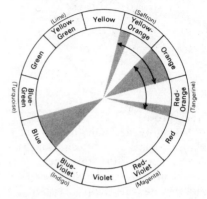

Adnate
Growing closely attached to an adjacent part or organ.
See also *Fasciated*

Advancing colours
Yellow, orange and red, 'active' colours which appear to come forward when contrasted with other colours. The use of these 'warm' colours helps to create depth in a design. See also *Receding colours*

Advent
The Christian season including the four Sundays preceding Christmas. Advent begins on St Andrew's Day (30 Nov) or on the Sunday nearest to it. Advent is the beginning of the Church's year.

Adventitious root
A root which develops from an un-usual part of a plant and other than on an existing root, eg on Ivy stems, on corms and bulbs and runners on Strawberry plants. The faculty to produce adventitious roots is

9

exploited when plants are propagated by means of stem cuttings or layering.

adventitious roots

Aerial root

A root growing from the part of a plant which is above the ground and does not root into soil. Such roots absorb moisture from the atmosphere and they may also help to support the plant.

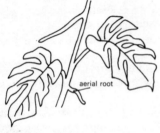

aerial root

Aerobic respiration

The commonest type of respiration where oxygen is used to break down carbohydrates. The result is chemical energy, carbon dioxide and water. See also *Anaerobic respiration*

Aesthetics

The study of the rules and principles of art as found in nature, the application of which result in perfect composition, harmony and unity.

Aestivation

The arrangement of the part of the flower bud especially the sepals and petals.

10

After-image

After visually concentrating on an area of intense colour and then closing the eyes, the same image in its complementary colour will appear. This is the result of the eye seeking restful reaction to an intense colour by absorption of the 'opposite' or complementary colour.

Also known as *accidental colour*.

Aggregate

A many-seeded berry which is fleshy, such as the Blackberry. Made up of many tiny drupes. See also *Drupes*

Air drying

A preservation technique; removing moisture from flowers either by natural drying or by accelerated drying in warm air. For some plants it is necessary to hang stems upside down to keep the tops rigid. Not a suitable method for preserving foliage.

Air layering

A means of vegetative propagation whereby roots are induced to form at nodes on a stem shoot. The stem is sliced half-way through longitudinally, then the cut is dusted with

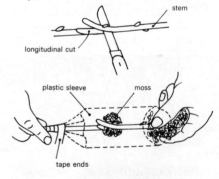

stem

longitudinal cut

plastic sleeve   moss

tape ends

hormone powder, wrapped around with damp moss and finally contained in plastic with the ends tied securely.

Air plants
Bromeliads that do not require to be in compost or soil and which grow on branches and trunks of trees, absorbing food and moisture through their leaves rather than their roots. In competitive floral art work they need not be in water or water-retaining floral foam.

Algae
A large group of simple, mainly aquatic plants having chlorophyll and other pigments but not true stems, roots or leaves. They may be single cell or multicellular.
The division includes seaweed. Previously classified in the Division Thallophyta.

Alginate
Soil conditioner made from seaweed and used to create a more crumbly texture on heavy soils.

Alkali soil
A soil with a pH higher than pH7 (which is neutral) and which supports a natural vegetation of beech, dogwood, hazel and old man's beard (clematis vitalba).

All-round design
Denotes a design or flower arrangement that is created to be viewed from all sides.

Allée
A walk bordered by trees or clipped hedges and whose base may be of gravel, turf or sand.

Allée en berceau
A short walk with overhead protection of climbing plants that are generally fragrant and trained over vault-shaped trellis work.

Allele
In most organisms there are two alleles (alternative form of a gene) and one from each parent occupying the same position on two homologous chromosomes. One allele is often dominant (the other recessive) and this determines the characteristic of the organism. It is an important aspect of plant genetics.
See also *F1 hybrids*

Allelopathy
One plant affecting another growing around it by discouraging growth through toxins in fallen leaves; or flowers being killed by the presence of ethylene gas.

Alternate
Leaves or other parts of a plant arising successively from a different level on the stem. See also *Opposite*

Amarantaceae P4-4 or (4-5) A4-5 G(2-3)
Family of Amaranthus, Iresine, Celosia.

Amaryllidaceae P3+3 A6 Ḡ(3)
Monocotyledon family including Nerine, Alstroemeria, Galanthus, Leucojum and Narcissus.

11

Amino acid

An essential component of proteins; some acids can be synthesized in plants from simple inorganic compounds.

Ampelidaceae K(4-5) C4-5 A4-5 G̲(2)

Family of woody climbers the most important being the Vine (Vitis). It includes Ampelopsis and Parthenocissus.

Anacardiaceae K(3 or more) C3-7 or o A5-14 G̲1

A family of trees and shrubs including the Rhus (Sumach) and Cotinus coggygria.

Anaerobic respiration

Respiration in which atmospheric oxygen is not used to break down carbohydrates, resulting in less energy than in aerobic respiration. The respiration of fungi is anaerobic. See also *Aerobic respiration*

Analogous colours

A related harmony consisting of three or four colours which are adjoining each other on the colour circle but which must *not* include more than one primary colour, eg, yellow/green, yellow, yellow/orange, orange.

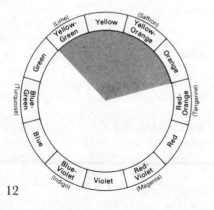

Analogous complementary colours

A contrasted harmony of four colours, three adjacent on the colour circle and one direct complement of *any* of them, eg yellow/green, yellow, yellow/orange and blue/violet.

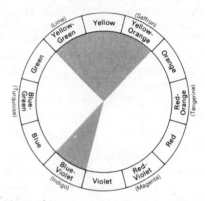

Anatomy

The science concerned with the physical structure of plants.

Androecium

The male sex organs (stamens) of a flower, the function of which is to produce the male gametes in pollen. It is the sum total of all the stamens in a flower structure. See also *Gynoecium*

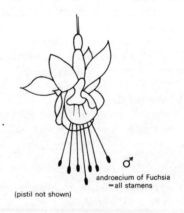

androecium of Fuchsia = all stamens

(pistil not shown)

Anemophily

Pollination of a flower by means of wind-carried pollen. Plants pollinated in this manner produce an enormous amount of pollen which is not usually scented. Grasses and most common British trees (except Limes) are wind pollinated.

Angiosperm

A subdivision of the Spermatophyta, a division of the plant kingdom. They are true land plants and are the dominant plant forms of the present day. Angiosperms are seed bearing and their ovules are enclosed in an ovary. There are two classes of angiosperms: monocotyledons and dicotyledons.
See also *Gymnosperm, Dicotyledon* and *Monocotyledon*

Annual

A plant that completes its life cycle in one year, ie it germinates, flowers, produces seeds and dies in twelve months or less. Annuals can be:
(1) *hardy* – sown where they are to flower and can withstand a certain amount of cold conditions;
(2) *half hardy* – raised in boxes in the greenhouse or frame, then hardened off and planted outside;
(3) *tender* (or greenhouse annuals). these require a warmer temperature than is afforded by outside climatic conditions.

Annual rings

Concentric rings in the cross-section of a trunk of a tree, each ring representing one year of growth. The width of the ring reveals the climate in the year it was produced.

Anther

The upper two-lobed part of a plant stamen, usually yellow in colour, in which pollen is produced within the two sacs on each lobe.

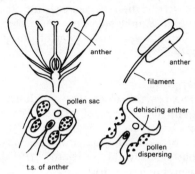

t.s. of anther

Apetalous

Flowers, without petals, which are often pollinated by the wind.

Apex

The tip of a shoot or root. The end of a leaf shape furthest from the point of attachment.

Apical dominance

Inhibition of the growth of lateral buds by the presence of a growing apical bud. Controlled by auxins and abscisic acid.

Apical meristem

Actively dividing cells in a region at the tip of each shoot and root of a plant producing new stem and root tissues.

Apocarpous

Separate carpels of a flower not joined together at their margins and typical of many primitive flowers.

Apocynaceae K(5) C(5) A5 G2
    or (2)

Small family, the stems of which have milky juice and which includes the Vinca.

13

Apomixis
A reproductive process in plants in which there is no fusion of gametes, no fertilization of pollen, and the ovules simply develop into seed. Almost a vegetative form of propagation.

Appliqué
The practice of cutting out designs from one piece of material and applying them to another to form a decoration. The material is usually, but not always, of cloth. A craft aspect of flower arranging.

Appressed
Leaves or suchlike pressed closely towards the stem; or lying flat or close against another part.

Aquatic plants
Plants adapted to live in water, most of which flower above the water's surface. Some live entirely submerged, others have flowers and leaves floating on the surface and others, such as a yellow flag iris, have most of their foliage above the surface.

Aquifoliaceae K4 C4 A4 $\underline{G}$(4)
The Holly (Ilex) family of about 300 species, many evergreen, most dioecious.

Araceae P4-6 or o A2-8 $\underline{G}$(1-3)
Monocotyledon family includes Calla, Lysichitum and Dracunculus.

Araliaceae K5 C5 A5 $\bar{G}$(5)
A family of trees and shrubs includes Aralia, Fatsia japonica and Hedera helix var.

Arboretum
A collection of many different species and varieties of living trees that are grown for scientific study and public exhibition. Well known arboreta in this country are at Westonbirt, Glos; Kew, Surrey; Wisley (RHS Gardens), Surrey; Bedgebury Pinetum, Kent; Bolderwood (New Forest), Hants.

Arbour
A shady garden shelter or bower often made of lattice work and covered with climbing plants. Sometimes part of a pergola.

Aril
A fleshy extra seed envelope, often coloured and partly covering a seed.

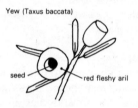

Yew (Taxus baccata)

seed — red fleshy aril

Arista
The tip of a leaf drawn out into a fine whisker-like point.

Aromatic
Distinctive, usually fragrant, scent; organic compounds in which carbon atoms are arranged in rings of six.

Arrangement
Something composed of various ordered parts as a result of arranging, viz flower arrangement.

In competitive work the term has been superseded by the word 'exhibit' but it remains in popular usage for general and non-competitive work.

Art Deco
An art style of interior decoration etc, which developed in the 1920s to the

1930s as a reaction to Art Nouveau. The principal characteristics are geometrical motifs and stylized natural forms adapted to mass production. It helped to popularize Cubism and Futurism art styles. The first exhibition of Art Deco was in Paris in 1925.

Art Nouveau

A decorative style which was common in interior design, graphic arts and fashion as well as architecture. The period lasted from 1880-1925. Art Nouveau owed its origins to William Morris and the Arts and Crafts Movement. Stylized and sinuous flowering plant forms dominate the style reflecting a deep interest in nature.

Artefact

An item or object of art or craftsmanship created by man (most commonly used in reference to archaeological finds).

Artificial key

A method of identifying plants by the process of elimination: first, the choice of at least two different characteristics then another choice, leading eventually to the correct identification.

Artificial plant material

Any manufactured replica or simulation of any type of plant material in any man-made substance (including silk or polyester flowers and foliage) and artificial turf/grass. All are expressly forbidden in competition work unless specifically allowed in a schedule.

Decorative plant material designs which are incorporated on containers, accessories, candles, bases or backgrounds are acceptable.
See also *Accessories*

Artificially coloured plant material

The technique of colouring material with special paints or spraying, dyeing, bleaching, staining or varnishing it for use in a more decorative manner. In competition work it is permitted unless expressly forbidden in show schedules.

Arts and Crafts Movement

Founded by William Morris around 1860 to revive the Guild system and create better conditions for craftsmen. It helped pave the way for Art Nouveau and beautiful designs.

Asexual reproduction

Multiplication of plants from one individual plant without the need for fusion of sex cells from different parents. The principal methods are by vegetative propagation, eg bulbs, corms, tubers and by spores.
See also *Vegetative propagation*

Assemblage

The creation of a work of art as a sculpture in 3D form by constructing or connecting 'found' objects. Its counterpart on a flat surface would be collage. A craft aspect of flower arranging. See also *Collage*

Assessment

The observation of students' achievement or progress on a course as related to the requirements of a syllabus. It can be mandatory, periodic or both.
See also *Evaluation* and *Judging*

Asymmetrical (botany)
Lacking symmetry; not symmetrical in respect of flower structure.
See also *Zygomorphic*

Asymmetrical balance
A design where visual stability is achieved by an equilibrium of visual weight without the use of regular or equal amounts of plant material on either side of an imaginary axis. The main axis is seldom emphasized. Asymmetrical balance, being more free and flexible, is favoured in most Modern and Abstract designs.

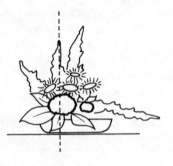

Atomiser
A device fixed on to the top of an enclosed bottle for reducing liquids to a fine spray. It is used for covering an arrangement with a fine mist of water in order to reduce transpiration, to spray rooted cuttings, to give a foliar feed to plants or to spray chemicals against pests and diseases.

Auricle
Small ear-shaped extension at the base of a leaf which curves back to the petiole (stalk).

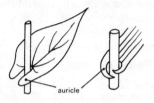

auricle

Authority
The name of the author who first gave a plant species its name. Usually expressed as a capital letter after the binomial, eg Achillea filipendula L. (Linnaeus).

Auxin
A general name for a group of plant growth substances which affect such processes as the growth of cell enlargement, apical dominance and root initiation in cuttings. Indole acetic acid is the most naturally occurring auxin.

Avenue
Drive or road leading to a large country house which is tree lined.

Awl-shaped
Tapering, often curved, and ending in a stiff slender point.

Axil
The point where the upper side of a leaf stalk (petiole) joins the stem and forms an angle. Axillary buds are those which develop in axils.

Axillary
Arising in the axil; also describes buds that are so formed. Axillary

buds which do not develop are said to be dormant.

Axis
The imaginary line running through the centre of a plant or any part of it. Also the imaginary vertical line through an arrangement which determines whether it is a symmetrical or an asymmetrical design. An axis can be horizontal or vertical and is related to good visual balance in designs.

B

Back-cross
The offspring of a hybrid crossed with one of the original parents of that hybrid

Background
A suitable backing behind an exhibit which must be free standing if provided by the competitor. Backgrounds must conform to space (measurements) allowed. If they are not permitted by a show committee then this should be stated in the schedule along with the details of any alternative background being provided.

Backgrounds should complement the design in both shape and finish. They can be integral with it and/or be a support for additional mechanics and drapes. Backgrounds play a more dominant part in Modern and Abstract work. An extra background may always be used unless prohibited in the show schedule.

Backing
The covering of the mossed base of a funeral tribute by foliage, (Laurel leaves or Cupressus), by wreath wrap, oiled paper, or polythene in order to neaten the finish of the underside. The use of floral foam in a plastic tray or base obviates the need for this type of backing.

Back spray head-dress
A head-dress for an adult bridesmaid

worn at the back of the head and only suitable for certain hair styles. It can be made up from mixed flowers but is specially suitable for the use of one type of flower, eg rose.

Balance
Considered as having two meanings:
(1) actual balance; achieving mechanical stability so that an exhibit does not topple over;
(2) a principle of design – visual balance; the placement of plant material in a design so that it does not appear top- or bottom-heavy or lop-sided.

Balance does not imply repose from lack of activity but suggests one visual force is holding another in a state of equilibrium.
See also *Asymmetrical, Dynamic, Static, Symmetrical balance* and *Balance by placement*

Balance by placement
Achieved when an arrangement is dependent on a base, an accessory or

its setting to complete the overall visual balance of the design and where on its own would otherwise appear unbalanced.

Ball

The compact mass of roots and soil around a plant in a pot. A root ball permits the lifting of a shrub or plant with a mass of roots and soil (which is then covered with sacking). This is an ideal way of transplanting such subjects in the appropriate season.

Balsaminaceae K3 C5 A5 G(3)

The Impatiens family of which tinctoria sp. thrives in protected warm corners in milder counties.

Bare-root stock

Plant material lifted without a root ball of soil – the manner in which roses, soft fruit and wallflowers are sold in autumn months. Roots must be protected from frost or prevented from drying out. Plants can be 'heeled-in' to await ideal planting conditions.

Bark

(1) A protective layer of mostly dead cork cells covering the outside of woody stems. The bark cambium includes the phloem and periderm.
(2) Thick cork bark is often used as a feature in some exhibits especially those with a landscape theme. It is natural dried plant material.

Bark ringing

The removal of two half-circles of bark about 13 mm wide, one 25 mm above the other on the trunk of a tree, in order to encourage fruit formation.

Basal

Attached to the base and not the apex, eg an ovule attached to the base of the ovary.

Basal rooting

A bulb which only roots from its base, such as European and American lilies.

Bascade, baskette, basquette

A bouquet or two corsage-type designs joined with a hooped handle which is carried by a small bridesmaid.

Base

Part of the staging of an exhibit or design which supports a container; or the whole area supporting the exhibit. Bases may be used singly or severally and are not considered an accessory. They can therefore be used even if accessories are not permitted.

A base should contribute more than simply serve to separate the exhibit from the table covering and should complement the design in shape, texture, colouring and size.

Base (in floristry)

A polystyrene base on which water-retaining floral foam is fixed. It can be in the shape of a wreath or heart, etc, and used as an alternative to wire frames. Bouquet bases are also available.

Basket

(1) A container made of interwoven strips of pliable material such as cane, straw, willow or thin wood, often carried by means of a handle and made in many shapes and sizes. In competitive work the basket must be made predominantly of plant material. If it has a handle it should be possible to pick the basket up

without damaging the plant material. If the basket has a lid then this should remain partly visible. Basket-type containers of any other materials can be used if permitted in the show schedule.

(2) A garden feature of baskets filled with flowers. Used by Repton as a grouping in isolation rather than spoil the landscape.

Batter

The sloping sides of a hedge created by having a narrow top and wider base; the angle of slope between the base and top of a dry-stone or retaining wall.

Bauhaus

School of architecture and design founded in 1919 by Walter Gropius (1883-1969) in Weimar (Germany). Influenced by the Arts and Crafts Movement. The school moved to Dessau in 1925 and Gropius resigned in 1928. In 1932 it moved to Berlin but it was closed in 1933 by the Nazis. Kandinsky and Klee were artists on the teaching staff.

Beaked

A carpel or fruit prolonged into a point.

Beard

Dense growth of (usually) yellow hairs occurring at the upper ends of the falls (lower pendulous petals) of flag irises.

Bed, bedding

Areas which are isolated from their surroundings, usually made in grassed areas in which a particular group of plants is cultivated, eg rose-bed.

Bedding is a system of planting beds with different subjects at different times of the year
Spring bedding – Wallflowers, bulbs and polyanthus,
Summer bedding – geranium, lobelia, petunias, etc,
Winter bedding – pansies, dwarf conifers and heathers.
See also *Carpet bedding*.

Bee bole

A recess in a thick garden wall in which straw bee-skeps were protected in winter.

Begoniaceae   P4 A ∞ and P5 $\bar{G}(3)$

Small family includes Begonia evansiana a hardy species but needing a sheltered corner.

Belt

Landscaping of trees round the perimeter of an estate, in some cases to provide shelter. Used in 18th-century English landscape in particular.

Berberidaceae   P4 or more A4-6 $\underline{G}1$

Largish family of woody and herbaceous plants including the Berberis, Mahonia and Epimedium.

Berceau

A form of trellis work over which climbing plants are supported. A feature of early French and Dutch gardens.

Berry

A fleshy fruit containing many, usually small, seeds embedded in pulp or formed from one carpel. The inner layer of the fruit wall is never hard and stony as in some drupes.
See also *Aggregate*.

Besom
A garden broom commonly made of birch twigs secured to a handle with a band of wire or, more traditionally, a cleft hazel-rod binding.

Best in Show
An award given to the most outstanding exhibit taken from all the first prizewinners in a show (unless some classes are expressly excluded from the award as stated in the show schedule).

Betulaceae   P4 or o A2-4 Ḡ2
A large family of trees and shrubs consisting of over a hundred species within the Birch, Alder, Hornbeam and Hazel family.

Biennial
A plant that requires two growing seasons in which to complete its life cycle. Sown, germinates and grows in the first year, flowers, reproduces and dies in the second year.

Bifid
Leaf divided or cleft into two parts or lobes.

Bignoniaceae   K(5) C(5) A4 G̲(2)
Family of woody and herbaceous plants includes the climber Campsis and Catalpa trees. The Incarvillea is the most familiar herbaceous subject.

Bilateral symmetry
Flowers which are symmetrical in one direction only (usually called *zygomorphic*).
See also *Actinomorphic* and *Zygomorphic*

Binding
The use of securing materials, wire, string, raffia, etc, for anchoring moss

to a frame in funeral work; the tying of plant materials for a presentation bouquet or adding ribbon to a bouquet handle.

Binding point (or tying point)
The point at which flower stems or wires are all joined together in a bouquet, corsage or other assembled design using silver reel-wire.

binding point

Binomial nomenclature
The system of naming and classification of plants using a two-part Latin name, established by the Swedish botanist Linnaeus (Carl Linné) 1707-1778. The first part is the genus, the second is species. Usually written in Italics thus: genus (*Fritillaria*), species (*imperialis*), authority (L = Linnaeus).
See also *Cultivar*.

Bipinnate
Compound leaves having both leaflets and stems bearing them arranged pinnately as in many ferns.

Bisexual

Organisms with both male and female reproductive organs on the same plant, ie a plant whose flowers contain both stamens and carpels.

Black

An achromatic (ie devoid of hue) colour consisting of equal mixtures of pigments of the three primary colours: red, blue and yellow. Black is not usually termed a colour though Ostwald claimed that since the subjective emotional value of black was as important as that of the chromatic hues, it should be considered as a colour. It is the complement of white, the other extreme of the neutral grey series.

Zodiac: Capricorn
Heraldry: Sable, Grief and Penitence
  effect under tungsten light: black
  effect under white fluorescent light: blue-black

Opt app	Psycho eff	Symb interp
dark	depression	mourning
heavy	deepening	death
deep	threatening	sorrow
dense	solemnity	evil
impenetrable	oppression	secrecy
lifeless		terror
gloomy		devil
sombre		mystery/ magic
		fear
		dignity

Blade

The whole leaf, excluding the stalk (petiole); all the parts of a leaf *except* the midrib (central vein). More generally applied to a narrow leaf such as grass, or daffodil, etc.

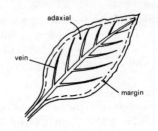

Bleaching

The treatment of wood or foliage by action of sunlight or chemical agents to lighten their colour. They are inclined to yellow slightly as a result.

Bleeding

The excretion of sap usually as a result of pruning late in the season; the cutting of stems of certain plant material especially Euphorbia which exudes a milky-white sap which can cause irritation to skin.
See also *Latex*

Blight

Any disease causing physical damage to plants which show up as being withered or shrivelled but without showing any signs of rotting.

Blind

A condition in which a plant has no growing point and will not produce flowers.

Bloom

(1) A solitary flower or composite head on one stem. A bud showing colour or a sufficiently open form is considered a bloom. See also *Flower*
(2) Fine whitish coating on the surface of fruits or leaves consisting of minute grains of a waxy substance, especially on those plants which like dry conditions. See also *Flower (2)*

Blossom
The flower or flowers of a plant especially those producing edible fruits; also refers to flowering shrubs; the period of flowering.

Blue
A primary colour, associated with the sky, water and brightness. It is said to be a favourite colour of the introvert as opposed to red which is a strong virile colour associated with the extrovert. It is a recessive or 'distant' colour and has a sense of being lightweight.

Zodiac: Sagittarius
Heraldry: Azure, Piety and Sincerity
  effect under tungsten light: greyish-blue
  effect under white fluorescent light: slightly brightened

Opt app	Psycho eff	Symb interp
clear	soothing	sky
cold	dreamy	sea
distant	refreshing	freedom
wet	tranquility	longing
fresh	clarity	infinity
pure	introspective	meditation
gentle		absorption
calm		sincerity
receding		faith
clean		immortality
lightweight		loyalty
		fidelity
		Jupiter

Blue-green (turquoise)
A tertiary colour obtained from the mixture of blue and green. The 'coldest' of all the colours.
Zodiac: Pisces   *Heraldry:* not used
  effect under tungsten light: slightly greyed
  effect under white fluorescent light: slightly greyed

Opt app	Psycho eff	Symb interp
cold	soothing	independence
distant	cooling	individuality
shady	subdued	idealism
watery	harsh	longing
icy/chilly	fascinating	lightweight

Blue-violet
A tertiary colour obtained from the mixture of blue and violet;
  effect under tungsten light: greyish-blue
  effect under white fluorescent light: slightly purple

Opt app	Psycho eff	Symb interp
clear	soothing	independence
full	reflective	loyalty
restful	concentrating	steadfastness
sober	restrained	
heavy	fortifying	

Bog garden
Artificially constructed garden in association with a stream or pool. The soil, kept permanently wet, is suitable for certain Primulae, water iris, Lysichitum, etc.

Bolt
When a vegetable plant starts flowering rather than make a good 'heart' it is said to 'bolt', especially lettuce in dry, hot conditions.

Bonsai
Japanese art of dwarfing trees by severe root restriction, pruning and pinching back growing shoots. Many local societies now cater for this expanding specialist hobby.

Boraginaceae   K(5) C(5) A5 G̲(2)
Mostly herbaceous plants which includes Anchusa, Borage,

Pulmonaria and Myosotis (Forget-me-not).

Border
A relatively narrow cultivated area of a garden running beside a path, fence, lawn or wall and planted up in many styles and flower subjects.
See also *Herbaceous border*

Bosquet
An ornamental grove or shrubbery designed either in geometric patterns or sinuous shapes.

Botany
A branch of biology which is concerned with living plants (organisms) and their scientific relationships, their structure and internal structure (morphology and anatomy) and their function and breeding (physiology and genetics).

Bottle cup
A shallow bowl-like container with a spiked screw in the base which can be screwed into the cork of a bottle. Available in 3 or 4 sizes of diameter.

Bottle garden
A particular form of indoor gardening where suitable plants are planted in large glass bottle jars (carboys). The glass provides some protection against draughts, fluctuating temperature, dust and insects and at

the same time provides some humidity as a micro climate.

Bottom heavy
Relating to visual balance where too much, or too dominant plant material is placed towards the base of the arrangement. It is a matter of good judgment to determine the fault and how to correct it.

Bouquet, formal
Natural flower material wired for support and arranged in any style for carrying by a bride or for formal presentation so that it can be carried in public. It can be arranged as a shower, crescent or semi-crescent design. Bridal bouquets can also be designed using fabric flowers.

Bouquet, informal

Natural flower materials on their own stems wired for support, if absolutely necessary, and in either a symmetrical or asymmetrical design. It is for presentation in public and to be carried. The recipient would expect to use the flowers at home afterwards. Also known as natural bunch or tied assembly.

Bowl

An hemispherical container which is wider than it is deep and made in many kinds of materials for displaying flowers in exhibition or in the home.

Box pleating

The edging of a formal funeral tribute design, usually in ribbon, in order both to protect the flowers and provide a finish.

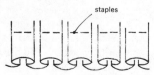

Bracket fungus

Fungus growing in the wood of living or dead trees producing flat-topped, sometimes large brackets on the side of the tree trunks.

Bract

Any leaf-like structure on the flower stalk outside the sepals and petals; describes small leaves at the axils from which flowers arise. Bracts are often brightly coloured, eg Poinsettia. In competition work bracts can be considered either as flowers or foliage but are discouraged in a class for foliage only.

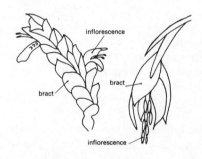

Bracteole

A small bract. See also *Bract*

Branch

The lateral shoot or secondary woody stem on the trunk of a tree; the subdivision of the stem or root of any other plant.

Branching unit

An assembly of materials of one kind and colour, the short stems of which have been taped. The materials are assembled with the smallest item at the tip and increasing in size as the unit is built up, leaving 'branches' of

25

stems in the design as it is made up.
See also *Ribbed unit*

Break
The appearance of a new shoot as the result of disbudding or removal of the growing tip thus encouraging new growth from the leaf axils.

Bridy holder
A plastic handle with a thin plastic 'cage' on top in which floral foam is inserted prior to assembling a bouquet.

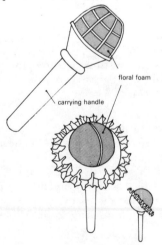

floral foam

carrying handle

Bridynette and posy holders also serve the same purpose for bridal and reception bouquets. All these are useful where delicate flower material is used because the flowers will last longer in water-retaining material. For all these types of holders decorative frills are available.

Broadcast
To sow smaller seeds as evenly as possible over a wide area, as opposed to sowing in drills.

Brown
A colour obtained by mixing red and yellow with blue or black. It has a fundamental quality, is the colour of the earth and it transmits stability. It is one of the colours of Autumn.
Zodiac: Gemini   *Heraldry*: not used
 effect under tungsten light: chocolate brown
 effect under white fluorescent light: yellowish-brown

Opt app	Psycho eff	Symb interp
dark	solid	reality
heavy	strengthening	determination
solid	soothing	earth
earthy	depression	wood
firm		
rugged		
warm		

Bryophyta
A division of the plant kingdom containing the mosses and liverworts which grow in damp habitats. Most bryophytes have no vascular system.

Bud
A condensed undeveloped shoot bearing small folded or rolled leaves and flower parts protected by scales. Terminal buds exist at the tip of a

stem (apical buds) or in the axils of leaves (axillary buds); an expanded and unopened flower not showing petal colour. *At this stage it is considered as foliage in an exhibit.*

Bud scales
The outermost protective covering for tender foliage leaves of a bud on a tree. Bud scales, as with foliage leaves, leave scars after they have been shed.

Budding
A method of grafting where the bud or scion is inserted into the stock so that their tissues intermingle. The bud develops into a shoot containing all the characteristics of its parent plant. Roses and stone fruits are propagated by budding.

Buffet d'eau
Ornamental gardening feature against a wall over which water flows into bowls or troughs.

Buffet table design
A design for an occasion at which guests serve themselves food from various dishes displayed on a long table. A suitable arrangement can be much larger than for a more formal luncheon or dinner party but care must be taken not to include flowers which shed pollen on to the food. The style of arrangement should reflect the setting and occasion.

Bulb
An underground rounded plant organ enabling it to survive from one growing season to the next. It is a modified shoot with a short flattened stem. A terminal bud is surrounded by thick fleshy swollen leaf bases for food storage and is covered by papery brown scale leaves. It propagates vegetatively but if only one bulb is formed it is called perennation. If two bulbs are formed it is both perennation and vegetative propagation. Bulbs are monocotyledons. Compare with *Corm*.

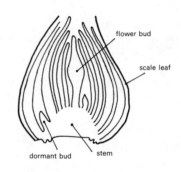

Bulbil
A small bulblike organ which may develop in place of a flower. Some lilies, notably L. tigrinium, produce bulbils in leaf axils. Treat as seeds for propagation.

Bun moss
Green, velvet-textured moss which is used to disguise mechanics in arrangements or to cover soil in a pot et fleur or planted bowl. It is also used as a foundation for some funeral designs.

Bundle sheath
A layer of cells around the vascular bundle in a leaf.

Bur
A seed vessel or flower head having hooks or prickles such as Acaena microphylla, Arctium spp. (Burdock).

Burning
The charring of stripped wood or teasels to give a charcoal or blackened look for dramatic effect.

Bush
A dense woody plant smaller than a tree with many branches arising from the lower part of the stem.

Buttonhole
A single flower or several flowers made up as appropriate to be worn on the lapel or in the buttonhole by gentlemen at weddings or other special occasions.

Two or more flowers can be made into a lapel spray for ladies.

Buxaceae ♂P4 A4 and ♀P6 $\underline{G}$(3)
Evergreen trees and shrubs with unisexual flower without petals; includes. Buxus (Box), Pachysandra, and Sarcococca.

C

C
The symbol for the corolla in the floral formulae (see also petals) eg cruciferae K4 C4 A4 + 2 $\underline{G}$(2) thus C4 = Corolla with 4 petals

Caesalpiniaceae K5 or (5) C5 A10 $\underline{G}$1
A sub-family of Leguminosae which includes Cercis and Gleditsia – a genus of extremely beautiful foliage trees, the best known of which is G. triacanthos 'Sunburst'.

Cake top
A design using fresh or fabric flowers placed on top of a wedding (usually tiered) or anniversary cake in either a silver trumpet vase, a floral foam pad or wine glass. The design should be light and dainty, in good proportion and in associated colours for the occasion.

Calcareous
Soils on limestone or chalk the substrates of which contain calcium carbonate ($CaCo_2$). Some plants will not tolerate such conditions due to the alkalinity and they are known as *calcifuge*.

Calcifuge
A plant which grows only or mainly on acid soil (or non-calcareous soil).

Callus
Hardened protective tissue consisting of parenchyma cells that develop over a wound or cut on a woody stem or damaged plant surface. When stem cuttings are taken a callus must form before it will root satisfactorily.

Calyx
The outer whorl of the perianth consisting of the individual parts known as the *sepals*. The floral formula for calyx is **K**.

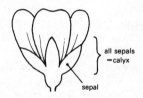

Cambium
Layer of actively dividing cells in the vascular system producing xylem on the inside and phloem on the outside. It is responsible for increasing the girth of the plant. Vascular cambium occurs in the stem and root.
See also *Cork cambium*

Campanulaceae K5 C(5) A5 G(2-5)
The 'Bellflower', large and beautiful family of flowers varying in size from 50 mm to 2.3 m. Includes Platycodon and Ostrowskia.

Campanulate
Shaped like a bell especially of flower corollas.

Canal

A water feature of French gardens in the 16th century for both ornamental appearance and practical purposes such as water storage and drainage. Very few examples exist in England but two notable ones are at Westbury Court, Glos (NT) and Wrest Park, Beds.

Candelabrum

(Candelabra = plural)

A decorative candlestick having several arms or branches for holding candles. A useful 'container' for some formal dinner arrangements using, for example, the centre (of three) cups in which candle cup and plant material is arranged appropriately.

Candle

A narrow cylinder shape of tallow, wax or other fatty substance containing a wick that is burnt to give light. They are elegant accessories providing line, colour, height and interest to many types of design and are obtainable in many shapes, sizes and colours. In competitive work candles are accessories but in the form of fruit and flowers are only allowed if the wick is showing.

Candle cone

An extending support for a candle which is shaped to a point for inserting into floral foam and is usually made of plastic.

Candle cup

Shallow, bowl-like container with short stem shaped like the base of a candle which fits into a candle-stick or candelabrum. It is available in several diameters and finishes, with domed or flat sides. It can also be secured into the neck of an empty bottle as an alternative to a bottle cup. See also *Bottle cup*

Candle-light

A subdued and very much a yellow light in its own right. The colours of an arrangement are affected by candle-light, eg, dark reds become almost black and purples lose their quality. The best colours to use are those with high luminosity, viz Yellows and Yellow/oranges. Whites tend to predominate in such light.

Capillary watering

Method of watering pot plants using the natural upward rise of water from a supply beneath the pots which percolates through the porous nature of the soil. Water is distributed evenly by means of a fine sand bed or capillary matting on which the pots are placed.

Capitate

Like a head; when many flowers are clustered together in an inflorescence.

Capitulum

A racemose inflorescence in the form

of a disc of sessile flowers, the youngest of which are in the centre. It occurs in the Daisy and Compositae family related plant.

Caprifoliaceae K(5) C(5) A4-5 Ḡ(2-5)

Mostly trees and shrubs: includes woody climbers (Lonicera). A large family whose flowers are usually scented. Abelia, Leycesteria, Sambucus, Symphoricarpos, Viburnum and Weigela.

Capsule

A dry fruit that releases seeds from several fused carpels when ripe which may be through splitting (dehiscent), viz

(a) lengthwise (eg Iris)
(b) pores at the top (Poppy)
(c) transverse lid (eg Plantain).

Carbohydrate

An organic compound containing carbon, hydrogen and oxygen. Starch and all sugars in which plants store the energy obtained from light during photosynthesis are carbohydrates.

Care card

A small card on which is printed a pithy description of various ways of improving the longevity of cut flowers or the care and maintenance of house plants.

Carmen rose

A rose made up of separate, suitably wired, rose petals surrounding a rose bud giving the appearance of a large 'blown' rose. It can be used as a corsage, attached to a handbag as an accessory or as a focal point in a formal bouquet. Also referred to as *Cabbage rose, Duchesse rose.*

Carnivorous

Half-hardy, herbaceous perennial plants with tubular-shaped reticulated leaves which are insect eating. Insects are attracted, then trapped and turned into nitrogen in order to feed the plant. This is done by the action of enzymes or bacteria. Although there are about 400 species the Venus fly-trap is the most commonly known. Commercial production of the Sarracenia sp. is now underway and the var. Leucophylla has a very attractive white leaf with green and red lining.

Carotenoids

A class of brown, orange and yellow pigments involved in photosynthesis but not directly in the capture of sunlight energy. Evident in such plants as golden Privet (Ligustrum ovalifolium var. aureum).

Carpel

The female reproductive organ of a flower consisting of ovary (with ovules) in the centre of the flower.

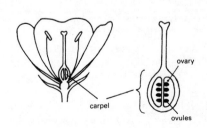

Carpet bedding

Fashionable Victorian art of using dwarf or creeping plants which could be trained in formal or geometric patterns into a carpet-like surface. The fashion lasted for only 20 years, 1860-1880, in private gardens but was part of Public park practice until the 1920s. It was emulated in Europe and the USA. See also *Bed, bedding*

Caryophyllaceae K4-5 or(4-5)
C4-5 A8-10 G̲(5)

A significant family which includes Dianthus, Silene, Lychnis, Arenaria, Cerastium and Gypsophila.

Catkin

A flowering stem, sometimes long, bearing many flowers adapted for wind pollination. Usually the male catkins hang down, the female is shorter and erect as in the hazel. In competitive work catkins are acceptable either as flowers or fruit at any stage of development.

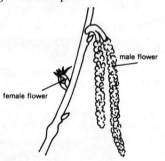

Celastraceae K4-5 or(4-5)
C4-5 G̲(2-5)

A family of trees, shrubs or woody climbers. Celastrus, and Euonymus and Pachystima.

Celebration

To have or organize festivities in order to mark special events such as a birthday or wedding anniversary – a joyous occasion.

Cell

A unit of protoplasm surrounded by a membrane. Plant cells have a nucleus, cell walls and plastids.
See also *Protoplasm*

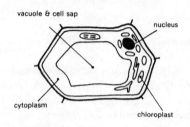

Cell division

The process whereby a cell divides to form two new cells, each containing a nucleus. Cell division can involve vegetative (asexual) or sexual reproduction.

Cell membrane

The membrane which encloses a cell.

Cell wall

The rigid wall, lying outside the membrane which surrounds a plant cell. Cell walls are made mainly of cellulose.
See also *Cellulose*

Cellulose

A carbohydrate polymer made of glucose molecules which is the most important substance in plant cell walls. See also *Cell wall*

Cereals

Grasses (Gramineae) producing edible grains; in competitive work they are acceptable as either flowers or fruit.

Chaplet

A memorial design/funeral tribute which has its origins in classical times when heroes were 'crowned'. It can be based with laurel leaves or cycas and can have a crescent bunch or anchor spray attached to the base. Large chaplets can be fitted with tripod legs for support at a memorial. Chaplets can also be finished with ribbons of military or ceremonial colours or emblems where required.

Charmille

A tall hedge, traditionally of hornbeam, close-clipped to give a wall-like appearance.

Chenille

A thick soft silk or worsted velvet cord or yarn covering a wire used for trimmings, the material being woven in tufts.

Chenopodiaceae P2-5 A = P G1

Apart from well-known plants belonging to this family such as Beet and Spinach, the important member for flower arrangers is Atriplex which has a striking silver-grey foliage.

Chiaroscuro

The use of light and shade, particularly in works of art where contrasts predominate (from Italian *Chiaro* = light, *obscure* = dark)

Chicken wire

A network of galvanised wire in differing sizes of mesh, usually supplied in rolls or cut lengths. It is either used in mechanics as additional security for water-retaining foam (by covering it with a neat parcel of chicken wire 25 mm mesh); or crumpled and used on its own or in conjunction with a pinholder to support, or help support, stems of flowers and foliage (50 mm mesh); or used on top of foam for swag work (12 mm mesh).
See also *Wire-mesh netting*

Chipboard

Rigid sheet made of compressed wood particles bonded with a synthetic resin; a useful material for backgrounds and base boards.

Chipping

The removal of a sliver of the outer hard seed coating to assist in its germination (as of Sweet Peas). The nick must be made opposite the hilum to avoid damage to the radicle.
See also *Hilum*

Chitting

The germination of seeds before sowing by placing them on moist felt or kitchen roll paper in warm conditions either prior to 'fluid drilling' or sowing singly.

Chlorophyll

Chemical (magnesium-containing) green pigments found in chloroplasts of all plants which use light energy for photosynthesis.
See also *Photosynthesis*

Chloroplasts
Green plastids containing chlorophyll, they are the site of photosynthesis, contain their own DNA and reproduce themselves.
See also *Plastid, Chlorophyll* and *Photosynthesis*

Chlorosis
The abnormal condition in leaves and stems of plants in which the chlorophyll is inhibited by lack of light, mineral deficiency or by viruses. The pale yellow coloration in the leaves is indicative of the condition.

Christmas
Christmas Day, 25 December, was fixed by the Church in AD 440 on the day of the winter solstice. The Anglo Saxon year began on that day. Supposedly the day on which Jesus Christ was born but the actual date is not known. Nevertheless a period of great rejoicing in the Church and a family festive occasion. Churches are decorated and flowers and pot plants are popular Christmas presents.
See also *Christmas decorations*

Christmas decorations
The whole gamut of festive arrangements for table decorations, garlands for doors, swags, crackers (with dried plant material attached) and holly wreaths for the home, etc. Churches are decorated specially for Christmas time and invariably have a crib and Christmas tree for the children. Red, green and gold are appropriate colourings for the season.

Chroma
The intensity, brilliance or dullness of a colour depending on the amount of achromatic (neutral) colour present.
See also *Achromatic colour*

Chromatic colour
Any hue, having chroma, that is derived from the visible spectrum. All colours, excluding white, grey or black are chromatic.
See also *Chroma* and *Hue*

Chromoplast
A plastid containing pigment. Chromoplasts give the autumn colours to leaves when pigments are present in larger numbers such as Red, Brown, Yellow.
See also *Plastid*

Chromosome
Threadlike bodies containing DNA, RNA and protein found in the nuclei of all cells. All the vegetative cells in a plant and in a species have the same number of chromosomes. They carry the genetic information in the form of genes. See also *Gene, DNA* and *RNA*

Ciliate
With a projecting fringe of hairs.

Circlet head-dress
A head-dress, usually for a child bridesmaid, which is made up from mixed fresh flowers and foliage, or fabric flowers, into a complete circle that sits well down on the head. It can be assembled as two units or one continuous circle.

Cladode
Flattened and modified stem resembling and functioning as a leaf such as Ruscus aculeatus (Butcher's broom).

Clair-voyée
Open panels of wrought iron-work or other kind of open-work fence, designed to give security without obscuring view. Much used in Dutch and French gardens and a feature of Westbury Court (NT), Glos.

Clamp
A frost-proof structure made of straw and covered with soil in order to store root crops during the winter.

Clasping base
Leaf base where there is no petiole; instead, the leaf clasps around the stem.

Class
A 'second order' category in the classification of plants in the Plant Kingdom and their grouping into orders and families.

Gymnospermae and Angiospermae are classes of the division Spermophyta. Dicotyledonae and Monocotyledonae and subclasses of Angiospermae.

Classification
The arrangement of a hierarchy of plants into groups from the Plant Kingdom down to species and variety.
See chart on back endpapers

Clone
A set of cells reproduced by vegetative means from the same original cell growing in many different places although genetically a single individual. Cultivars are usually clones.

Clump
Mass of matted roots, rhizomes or young shoots of an herbaceous plant. When lifted, can be divided as a means of vegetative propagation.
See also *Division*

Cluster
When two or more leaves, flowers, or fruits arise from the same point at the end of a main stem or of a side shoot they are said to be in a cluster.

Cluster head-dress
Somewhat dated style of head-dress suitable for bride or adult bridesmaid. Sometimes made up with mixed flowers but is better with one kind of flower. The clusters are positioned either side of the head.

Cocktail sticks
Short thin wooden (or plastic) lengths, sharpened both ends, which are used for a variety of purposes such as securing two or three pieces of floral foam together. Four may be fixed to the bottom of a candle to support it in floral foam, or anchoring fruit (eg apples) together in an arrangement.

Coffin spray (double-ended spray)
An informally designed funeral

35

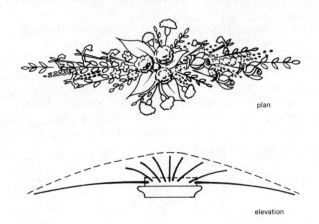

plan

elevation

tribute, usually as a family tribute placed on the coffin and carried with it. It is double-ended, viewed from all angles and at eye level. The two 'ends' need not be identical but the tribute is an important one and is generally lavishly executed in a good design.

Collage

Term derived from the French *coller* (to stick). A craft of the twentieth century, developed by the Cubists (Picasso and Braque in 1912) and also playing a part in Futurism. Earliest examples found in Japan in twelfth century, and in 1686 a handbook for cut-out silhouettes was published in Holland.

In floral art it is an abstract design or assembly of plant material either fresh or preserved (or both) with or without accessories fixed with adhesives on a visible background. The design should empha-size texture and three dimensional effects. May be expressive or non-objective and mounted in a frame or left unframed. A craft aspect of flower arranging. See also *Plaque*

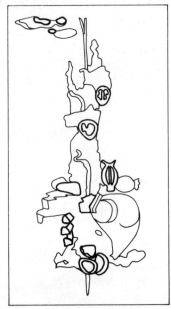

Collage in dried plant material (after Edna M Cordon)

Collenchyma

The cellulose tissue of cells for strengthening cell walls or at their corners especially – its primary function being support.

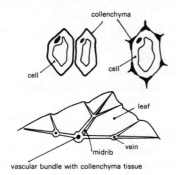

vascular bundle with collenchyma tissue

Colonnade

Architectural term used in the sense of topiary art where clipped Hornbeam, Thuja or Box are fashioned into columns.

Colour

A physical phenomenon produced by the decomposition of light and describes any visual sensation or effect of colour wave-lengths, including all gradations from white to black. Colour has three definite qualities or dimensions:

Hue – the name
Value – lightness or darkness
Chroma – intensity, brilliance or dullness.

Colour is an element of design in floral art.

The colour spectrum was discovered by Sir Isaac Newton in 1666.

Colour accent

The predominant colour of an arrangement – achieved by allowing greater use and emphasis of a selected colour especially in the focal area.

Colour association

Colours linked with moods, feelings, emotions, etc, eg Pink = feminine, Green =envy, Blue = depressed

mood or 'blue with cold'.

See also *Psychological effect* and *symbolic interpretation* for each specific colour

Colour circle (or wheel)

A diagrammatic means of depicting primary, secondary and tertiary colours and relationships in segments of a circle. Concentric circles show pure hue, tints, tones and shades of twelve colours. The 'opposites' are complementary colours, etc. There are many variations for the design of a colour circle.

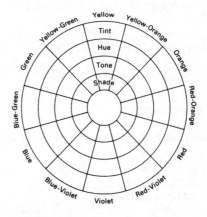

Colour discord

Colours which are generally not close enough on the colour wheel (or circle) for harmony, or not far away from each other for contrast, produce a discordant note and do not associate well together.

Red/orange (Tangerine) and Red/violet (Magenta) clash in this way.

Colour harmony

The unification of colour aspects so that the design achieves the intended result whether the harmony is analogous, complementary or monochromatic.

Colour intensity

A colour is most intense or saturated when it is pure and without any achromatic colour.

See also *Saturation* or *value (of colour)*

Colour juxtaposition/ simultaneous contrast

Colours change visually when influenced by other colours surrounding them or close by.

(1) A hue appears more saturated when placed near or next to its complement.

(2) A hue appears to alter when placed near or on one of its analogous hues.

(3) A dark hue on a light back ground will advance more than a bright hue on the same background (regardless of colour 'temperature').

Colour key

The dominant tonal value and colour intensity of a flower arrangement, picture, bouquet, etc.

See also *Low-key* and *High-key*

Colour-reaction

A black line around a superimposed colour on a background appears to make the colour richer and clearer by separating it from the background whereas a white or lighter colour outline has an opposite effect making the superimposed colour appear paler.

Colour response

A personal experience but the following have universal acceptance:

warm colours – joy, gaiety
cool colours – restful, soothing
light values – contentment
dark values – mystery, gloom
intense full chroma – nervous tension, restlessness

tints – weak, feminine
shades – sombre
tones – dignity
strong contrasts – excitement
related colours – calming effect
full chroma – strong, masculine.

See also *Symbolic colour*

Colour rhythm

The grading of the values of a dominant colour in shade or tint sequence in a successive range of lightness or darkness.

Colour temperature

A related association; warm colours are orange and red and 'advance' visually. Cool colours are green and blue and 'recede' visually. The 'temperature' is increased if a warm colour is placed next to a cool one and vice versa.

Columnar

Tall and narrow with straight sides; describes shapes of some trees.

Companion cells

Cells within phloem tissues of plants, closely associated with sieve tubes, and are small, narrow cells.

See also *Phloem*

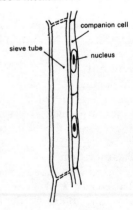

Compatibility

(1) Ability to exist together harmoniously. An exhibit or arrangement that, together with its component parts, quality of design, and formality (or informality) will be able to harmonize (or be compatible) with its setting.

(2) In pollination, *cross-compatibility* is shown where two varieties set seed when pollinated. *Self-compatibility* is shown when a variety sets seed with its own pollen.

Complementary colour

Two colours directly opposite each other on the colour circle forming a harmony. They are contrasting harmonies viz:
(a) Yellow and Violet
(b) Red and Green
(c) Blue and Orange
(d) Yellow/green and Red/violet
(e) Blue/green and Red/orange, etc.

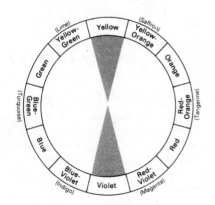

Components

The various parts or objects of an exhibit or arrangement which go to make up the whole design. The base, the container, the accessories, etc, are components of a design.

Compositae   K rudimentary or
   pappus C(5) A(5) Ḡ(2)

One of the largest families (13 tribes) of dicotyledons having composite inflorescences as in Daisies, etc. The blooms appear to be single flowers whereas they are composed of many tiny florets crowded on to a single receptacle.

Composition

The arrangement of artistic parts so as to form a unified whole that also harmonious. See also *Golden section*

Compost

Mixture of various ingredients specially prepared for sowing seeds or planting. It can contain loam and peat or be loam-less (entirely peat). John Innes compost (in various grades) is strictly formulated, and quality controlled for specific uses such as seed sowing, potting-on, etc. Not to be confused with the preparation of a vegetable waste-matter 'compost heap'.

Compound

A leaf form where the blade is divided into two or more separate leaflets, each with its own stalk and without buds in the axils: (1) compound palmate, (2) compound pinnate.

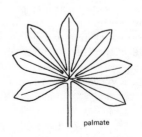

palmate

continued...

Compound
continued

pinnate

Concentration

The amount of a substance dissolved in a given volume of liquid. Expressed as parts per million, percentage or other liquid measurement ratios.

Condensation

Occurs where there is a marked difference between external and internal temperatures causing beads of moisture to form on glass. Its control is an aspect of greenhouse management.

Condition

The quality and physical state of plant material which should always be free from disease and malformed shapes and anything that detracts from the natural beauty of the flowers and foliage.

Conditioning

The careful treatment of fresh cut, living, plant material in order to preserve freshness and to prolong its life by various means so that stems take up water more easily.

The nature of the plant material determines how it has to be conditioned, viz woody, hard, soft, milky, hollow stems.

Cone

(1) Metal or plastic tubes shaped as inverted cones which are filled with water and which extend the height of an arrangement. They should be fixed securely to cane supports, or when spiked into floral foam they should be made quite stable before use.

(2) Conical, round, or cylindrical structures borne by certain trees such as pines, firs and cypresses and which are their reproductive structures, protecting the naked ovules by stiff woody scales. Used extensively in Christmas decorations.

Conic

Tapering evenly from base to apex.

Conifer

Trees or shrubs bearing cones, and members of the gymnosperm group. Mostly evergreen but exceptions are the larches, the Dawn Redwood and Swamp Cypress. They range from enormously large trees to very low-growing dwarf forms.
See also *Cone (2)*

Conformity

Compliance with the standards and rules as set in competitive work where it is necessary to apply correct specifications for style, period, size, Abstract, Still Life, etc, as well as measurements of space allowed in show classes.

See also *Not according to schedule*

Connate
Leaf base closely joined or united by growth.

Conservatory
A glass and wood or iron construction usually built so that it could be entered directly from the house and acted as a 'winter garden'. Interest in this Victorian fashion has been renewed and the conservatory is becoming popular again.

Container
A vessel or receptacle holding plant material. It may be a feature of the exhibit or be completely hidden. Containers can be fashioned from any substance and be of home-made manufacture. A container can vary from a simple tin can to an elaborate alabaster ewer. It should always be non-porous.

Container-grown plants
Plants grown in polythene or rigid plastic pots (generally not clay ones). The advent of the Garden Centre introduced container-grown stock which can be planted any time of the year (except in frosty conditions) enabling all year round sales. The idea originated in the USA.

Contemporary design
Two divisions of 20th century floral art based on the particular type of construction.

(1) *Radial structure:* with an area of interest at or near a single point of emergence with interest tapered to the outer edges includes Traditional. Modern, Free Style.

(2) *Interest equated:* with emphasis equated over the whole, no single point of emergence or focal area emphasized. Includes Abstracts, Mobiles, Avant garde, etc.

Continental design
A mainland European style of floristry or flower arranging some aspects of which are now influencing British designs. It is more 'Modern' in approach and uses exciting plant material.

Contractile root
A modified adventitious root developing from the base of a bulb or corm. Since a new bulb or corm develops above the old one, contractile roots shorten and draw the new corm down to the proper level below the soil.

Contrast
Different or opposite. In floral art it means placing the elements and using principles of design in such a way as to emphasise the differences, eg contrasting colours, shapes, texture, sizes, etc. Contrast in a design adds richness and impact through contradiction. Contrast is a principle of design. See also *Dominance*

Contrive
To adapt ingeniously; to fabricate; applies to the manipulation of plant material into un-natural shapes or forms.

Shaping leaves, folding, pinning and stapling are some methods. Also applies to made-up flowers which should comprise natural plant material and be recognizable as such. See also *Made-up plant material*

'Cool' colours
The blue and green range of colours. See also *Colour temperature*

Coral
A soft-bodied marine animal which builds itself a protective chalky skeleton. In large colonies it forms reefs. If used in exhibits it must be considered as an accessory. See also *Sea fan*

Cordate
Leaf bases signifying heart-shaped form.

Coriaceous
Leathery in appearance or resembling texture of leather.

Coriariaceae K5 C5 A5+5 G5
The family contains only one Genus of small shrubs – Coriaria, which are interesting because of their frond-like leaves especially C. *terminalis*.

Cork
Used in prefabricated form and shaped as bases for appropriate arrangements; natural pieces are used as an accessory or embellishment for Pot et Fleur work.

Cork (phellem)
A tissue of dead cells with suberin cell walls forming a protective waterproof layer. See also *Cork cambium*

Cork cambium (phellogen)
A type of cambium within the outer layers of the stems of woody plants making a protective ring surrounding the inner tissues. Cork cambium cells divide to produce phellem, an inner secondary cortex (phelloderm) in the process of secondary thickening.

Corm
A thickened stem base swollen with food reserves covered with a membranaceous protective sheath. They are organs of vegetative reproduction, eg Crocus, Gladiolus, etc, (compare with bulb). See also *Contractile root*

Cornaceae K4-10 C4-10 A4-20 $\bar{G}$(1-2)
An extensive family of 'Dogwoods' which range from creeping shrubs to trees. Cornus, Corokia, Davidia, Garrya elliptica, Griselinia littoralis and Aucuba japonica are examples.

Corn dolly
A decorative figure or emblem made by plaiting straw. Formerly used at

Harvest Festival time to grace the church door. Originated in the ritual of cutting the last corn of the harvest which was fashioned into an effigy or doll in which the spirit could take refuge. Kept during the winter and protected, it was then broken open in the spring to release the spirit into the sowing of new seed.

In competition work it is made-up plant material and an accessory.

Corolla

The petals of a flower forming the inner whorl of the perianth and encircling the carpels and stamen. The floral formula for corolla is C. See also *Petals*

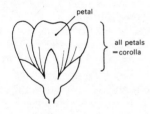

Corona

The appendages of petals or perianth which together form a ring around the centre of the flower, eg trumpet of a daffodil.

Coronet

A head-dress style for a bride. Many patterns can be created and are best made up with one kind of flower.

Corsage

Flowers, or flowers with foliage, wired and assembled. It is worn on the lower part of the shoulders of a dress or coat. It may be composed of one or two flowers or elaborately worked, depending on the occasion. There are many corsage shapes: round, triangular, Hogarth, crescent, pennant oblong, jabet, straight, L-shaped, etc.

Cortex

The tissue between the vascular system and the epidermis in plant stems and roots, composed of parenchyma and collenchyma cells. See also *Stem* and *Root*

Corymb

A type of flowering shoot (inflorescence) whose lower stalks are longer than the upper ones such that the inflorescence has a flat top and the outer (periphery) flowers open first.

Corymbose
Having flowers in corymbs.

Cotyledon
The part of the embryo of a seed plant. Some plants such as a bean have large cotyledons which store food and on emergence serve as first foliage leaves.
See also *Angiosperms, Monocotyledon* and *Dicotyledon*

Creativity
Imagination made visible; distinguishes an art from a craft. Techniques can be taught but imagination or insight cannot. It is not imitation it is origination.

Creeper
A plant incapable of supporting itself which usually has little or no secondary thickening in its stems.

Cremation basket (or sympathy basket)
A funeral tribute which is made up of fresh flower material, with or without foliage, arranged in a shallow basket which is flat and rectangular and lined with a watertight insert. The basket has a carrying handle.

Crenate
Leaf margins with broad based rounded teeth appearance.

Crescent
Any shape or form resembling the biconcave shape in the first or last quarters of the moon – often considered in flower arranging as the crescent line which is a segment of a circle.

Crescent bouquet
Can be a semi-crescent design or a full crescent the latter using more materials. A crescent is one third of a circle. The semi-crescent design can curve to the right or left but it should be a definite curve emphatic both at the trailing end and at the return end.

A full crescent design is made up of two main trails bound together at the centre of the design and the larger flowers in the focal area mounted and wired in separately.

Crinkle-crankle wall

See *Serpentine wall*

Crocks

Pieces of broken clay flowerpot used to provide drainage in seed boxes and pots. Large pieces cover the drainage holes concave downwards and smaller pieces provide an extra drainage structure.

Cross

A symbolic and traditional shape worked on a wire frame for a funeral tribute. Frames available in several sizes the largest being suitable for a coffin cross. Cross frames can be worked loose as well as foundation work. Crosses are also available in foam-based material. A spray of flowers can be added at the centre of the cross or at the foot to give an added dimension.

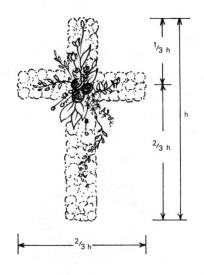

Cross-fertilization

Fertilization of a female gamete of one plant by a male gamete from another.

Cross-pollination

The pollination of one plant with pollen from another individual plant.

Crown

That part of perennial plants where stem and root meet and from which new shoots form and roots appear.

Cruciferae K4 C4 A4+2 $\underline{G}(2)$

A very large family consisting almost entirely of Herbaceous plants and includes Cheiranthus, Lunaria, Crambe, Iberis and Hesperis. Many plants have a rich vitamin content and family includes cabbage and kale, brussels sprouts, turnip, swede, radish and watercress.

Cubism

A radical revision of 20th century art in the belief that a painting is primarily an object. Essentially conceived by Picasso and Braque, Cubism is based on the fact that an object changes shape as it is looked at from different angles and different planes. Varying angles and planes are blended into one.

Cultivar

Relatively new technical term to describe variety of plant that has been developed as the result of horti-cultural practices. Derived from *culti*vated *vari*ety, eg 'White Swan'.

Cuneate

Leaf base ending in wedge shape.

long   narrow   broad

45

Cupule

A cup-shaped membraneous structure formed from bracts such as the base of an acorn.

Cushion

A formal massed design funeral tribute made from a wire frame in two sections, a base which is flat and a top which is curved with a wider mesh to contain the mossing. Available in various sizes and foam bases are often used as an alternative.

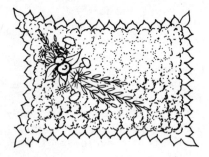

Cuticle

The protective layer of cutin on the surface of leaves which prevents both evaporation and protects the plant from disease.

Cutin

Waxy substance covering the outer surfaces of plant cells which is the main constituent of the cuticle. Cutin helps reduce water loss and prevents the entry of disease.

Cutting

Any severed part of a plant used to propagate a new plant (vegetatively). There are many types of cuttings. See under different headings, eg *Root cuttings*

Cuttings, Irishman's

A cutting consisting of already rooted stem or sucker which is severed from the clump. Chrysanthemums and Delphiniums can be propagated in this way.

Cyme

Type of flowering shoot (inflorescence) in which the first formed flower develops at the top of the main axis and prevents further growth of new flowers at the tip so that other flowers are produced from lateral buds beneath.

Cytoplasm

All parts of a cell outside the nucleus and inside the cell membrane. It is part of the 'living' part of the cell and all kinds of changes take place within the cytoplasm to ensure plants have air and minerals.

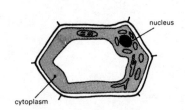

D

Dada
The expression coined by the Rumanian poet Tristan Tzara who said Dada 'signifies nothing'. Nevertheless it developed as an artistic philosophy and as a protest movement in Zürich in 1916. Jean Arp (1887-1966), Marcel Duchamp (1887-1968), Max Ernst (1891-1976) were notable exponents.
The Surrealist movement emerged after the demise of Dada.

Damping-down
Applying water in the form of a spray to paths or gravel floors under glass in order to raise air humidity during the day time in sunny weather.

Damping off
Collapse and death of young seedlings due to soil borne fungi invasion at soil level. It can be prevented by various chemical treatments and by sowing seeds thinly.

Dead-heading
The removal of dead flowers from certain plants in order to prolong the flowering season and in a few instances induce a second flush of flowers. It prevents seed formation. Roses should be dead-headed as should Lilac and Rhododendrons.

Decay
The process of decomposition or rotting involving the breakdown of organic compounds in the organism by bacteria and fungi. It takes place after the death of an organism and is an important part of the cycle in the ecological system.

Deciduous
Trees and shrubs shedding all or most of their leaves at certain times of the year (usually autumn and winter) in order to eliminate loss of water through transpiration or prevent damage in their dormant season from frost or drought.

Decorative
Serving to adorn; be ornamental; describes component parts of an exhibit which do not express any particular idea or theme. Beauty for beauty's sake.

Decorative Abstract (non-figurative)
A design concept where the result is non-objective and is a composition of shapes, colour, texture and forms of plant material used in a non-naturalistic manner. Plant material has to predominate and if fresh, must

be in water or water retaining material. Category no longer differentiated in Abstract classes.

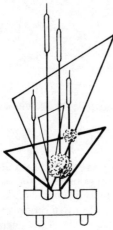

Découpage
From the French 'to cut out'; the craft of decorating furniture or objects by applying paper cutouts. Can be either two-dimensional or three-dimensional. A craft aspect of flower arranging.

Decumbent
Stems prostrate but with tip growing upwards.

Decurrent
A leaf base prolonged down the stem forming a wing or ridge.

Deficiency
The lack of a nutrient or nutrients without which plants lack growth and are prone to disease.

Mineral deficiency is indicated in various ways, eg the pale yellow colour of young leaves indicates an iron deficiency.

Defoliation
Stripping or removing leaves from stems of flowers either prior to conditioning or in order to retain flowers only. Some flowers do not last well unless all leaves are removed, eg Syringa (lilac) Philadelphus (mock orange blossom), etc. Defoliation also reduces transpiration.

Dehiscence
The spontaneous and sometimes violent splitting of a seedpod to release seeds, eg Iris foetidissima or Impatiens (seed dehiscence); or anthers to release pollen.

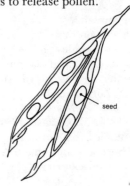
seed

Deltoid
Triangular shaped.

Dentate
Leaf margins with broad triangular teeth.

Denticulate
Minutely dentate, ie finely toothed leaves.

Depth
Achieving the illusion or actual direction into the third dimension. The use of component parts as well as plant material can be employed to create depth, including contrasts of warm (advancing) and cool (receding) colours, changes in texture, variations of shadow and reflective backgrounds. See also *Recession*

Desiccant
A substance (powder or crystals) that absorbs many times its own weight of water. Used as a drying agent in the preservation of flowers. Alum, borax, sand and silica-gel are the desiccants in use for preserving flowers.
See also *Silica-gel*

Design
Superseded by the word exhibit in the making of show schedules but applicable to wording assessments and judging criteria. A good design results from composition and utilization of the principles and elements of design.
See also *Elements of design* and *Principles of design*

Design function
The object or *raison d'être* of a design; to convey a message or interpretation; to be a pedestal for a wedding or a hospital locker arrangement, etc.

Development
The changes of structure and appearance of new growth in a plant.

Diadelphous
Describes either stamens that are united by their filaments into two bundles or one free stamen and the rest united.

Dibber
A wooden or plastic tool for making holes. Either a thick one for transplanting large plants in the garden or small and thin for inserting seedlings in trays.

Dichasium
A cymose inflorescence where two branches grow out from below the first flower and in turn these terminate in a flower and so on. Dichasium can be simple or compound. See also *Monochasium*

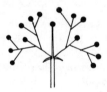

Dichotomous
Type of branching in plants when the growing bud (apical bud) divides into equal growing points and these in turn subdivide recurrently into two parts.

Dicotyledon

A class (Dicotyledoneae) of the sub-division of Angiospermae. Dicotyle-don embryos have two seed leaves within. Dicotyledons have secondary thickening in the stems, veins in their leaves in the form of a net, and vascular bundles in the stem. In the

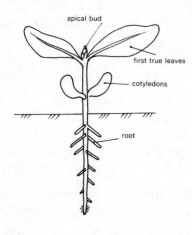

point at the end of a common stalk and which is divided like the fingers of a hand, eg Horse Chestnut, Japanese Maple, Helleborus foetidus.

roots of dicotyledons there are only ever 4 or 5 groups of Xylem and Phloem. On germination of the seed the cotyledons usually push up to the light and appear as first leaves.
See also *Monocotyledon*

Didynamous

Flowers with two long and two short stamens as in the foxglove.

Differentiation

The changes from simple more complex forms through the develop-ment of tissues and organs that become specialized for particular functions.

Digitate

A compound leaf in which 2, 4 or more leaflets arise from the same

Dioecious

Plant species that have male and female flowers on separate plants and require both to be grown in proximity in order to bear berries, eg Skimmia japonica and some forms of Ilex (Holly).

Diploid

Having two full sets of chromosomes in their nuclei. See also *Haploid*

Dipping well, pool or tank

A well, small pool or lead tank for dipping into for watering purposes. Used extensively in gardens designed by Lutyens and Gertrude Jekyll.

Dipsacaceae   K(4-5) C(4-5) A4 G(2)

Small family includes both the teasel and Scabious.

Direct line

A solid, tangible line, without repetition of form or points, causing eye movement more strongly than by any other shape.

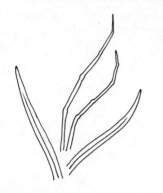

Disbud
The removal of unwanted buds from stems or cuttings either to train plants or to improve the size and quality of main bloom on a plant, eg Chrysanthemum

Disk
Flat circular receptacles such as those on the Compositae family.

Disk-floret
A flower in the central part of a composite inflorescence.

Dispersal
The movement of seeds away from the parent plant by a variety of mechanisms including wind, birds, water, mammals and self-dispersal, eg Gorse.

Dissected
Divided into many narrow segments.

Distichous
Leaves arranged in two vertical rows on opposite sides of the stem.

Distinct
Separate; not united even at extreme base; refers to classification of varieties.

Distinction
The sum total of all the design qualities of an exhibit which sets it apart from all others and which in itself has distinguishing features and a degree of excellence.

Divaricate
Branches that diverge at a wide angle, forked, spreading far apart.

Divergent
Separated and going in different directions from a point.

Divided
Separated into lobes or segments with spaces between.

Division (botany)
A 'first order' category in the classification of plants in the Plant Kingdom that consists of one or several similar classes. Division names end in -phyta, eg Bryophyta (mosses and liverworts). Pteridophyta (clubmosses and Ferns). Spermatophyta (gymnosperms and angiosperms).

Division (horticulture)
Multiplication or rejuvenation of plant material by splitting the crown of a plant, by separating rhizomes or clumps as a means of vegetative propagation.

DNA
Deoxyribonucleic acid, chief constituent of chromosomes. Can replicate itself, and transmits genetic information by genes from parent to offspring.

Dominance
Having primary control or influence

51

over something; synonymous with emphasis and focus and is based on unequals; implies some subordination in the design. Dominance is achieved where one line, one shape, one colour, one texture plays the major, commanding role. Dominance is a principle of design.

Dominant (botany)

A genetic term describing the allele that functions when two different ones are present in the cells of an organism.

Dormancy/dormant

The inactive period in the life of seeds or plants during which annuals survive the winter as seeds and many perennials survive as dormant tubers, bulbs or rhizomes; not grow-ing; a reduced state of metabolism. Axillary buds which do not develop are also termed *dormant*.

Dorsifixed

Describes an anther attached to its filament at the back and not at the extreme lower end.

Dot plant

A single specimen plant featured in a formal flower bed in order to create contrast in height and colour against smaller bedding plants.

Double

Flowers with more than the usual number of petals, often with the style and stamens changed to petals.

Double internal wiring

Method of wiring a flower stem by inserting one wire up to the flower head (giving it support but no anchorage) and inserting a second

wire as far up the stem as possible in order to wedge the first wire securely.

Double-leg mount

The addition of a wire to the base of a stem for anchorage into a wreath or bouquet so that after inserting wire to stem, bending into hairpin shape and winding wire to stem, two wires of equal or almost equal length protrude beyond the stem end.

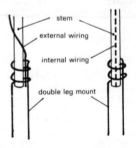

stem
external wiring
internal wiring
double leg mount

Double serrate

Leaf margin where large teeth and small teeth alternate.

Dovecote

Originally serving the utilitarian purpose of providing food in the Middle Ages (Pigeons), they became an ornamental garden feature in 17th-18th century estates when farming methods had improved.

Drape

An appropriate fabric of any kind which is arranged behind an exhibit to complement, contrast or be incorporated into the design. May be used unless prohibited in the show schedule. A drape is not an accessory.

Drawn

Plants or seedlings which are thin and weak as the result of over-crowding or having been grown away from natural light conditions.

Dried plant material

Any plant material which has been preserved by drying, bleaching, glycerining, pressing, desiccating or skeletonizing; includes wood, roots and bark.

In competitive work, made-up plant material is acceptable if component parts are of dried plant material and used in an appropriate class for it.

See also *Bleaching, Glycerine, Pressing, Desiccant* and *Skeletonizing*

Dried wood

Alternative classification for driftwood; excludes spathes and exotic seed pods in competitive classes.

Driftwood

Wood washed up by the sea, lake or river but now includes any type of dried wood, (branches, roots or bark)

in competitive work. It can be treated or finished by artificial means (as well as by bleaching or waxing). Driftwood is a dried plant material and not an accessory. See also *Dried wood*.

Driftwood holder

Various patterns of a clamp on a heavy lead base with or without an inverted pinholder. Also a heavy lead base with an inverted screw which is inserted into the base of driftwood to give stability.

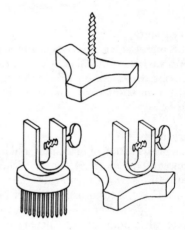

Dri-hard

Clay impregnated with a nylon filament and which is malleable, provided it is kept moist and wrapped. Hardens on exposure to atmosphere. It is used as a base for dried arrangements where permanence and more security are needed. Available in Green and Brown colours (Trade name).

Drill

A narrow, straight furrow in which seeds are sown outdoors. They can be taken out by the back of a drawhoe, rake or stick. The depth of drill must be appropriate to the size of seed to be sown.

Drupe

Fleshy indehiscent fruit developing from one carpel in which the seed (kernel) is enclosed in a hard shell, eg Plum, Cherry.

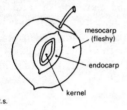

t.s.

Dry goods

The many stock items of a florist's shop such as containers, accessories, ribbons, wires, care cards, greetings cards, sympathy cards and wrapping paper.

Drying

The preservation of plant material by removing the moisture content either naturally or with chemicals. 'Dried flowers' is the term used to cover all forms of preservation of plant material. Conditions for drying are usually a dark, dry and fairly cool environment. A variety of flower stems are hung upside down in suitable bunches for natural drying techniques.

Dry pack

Florist's flowers and foliage that have been packed and despatched after being harvested without an initial plunge in water. Such plant material needs an additional day's conditioning before arranging or selling.

Duchesse rose

See *Carmen rose*.

Dwarfing root-stock

Root stock inducing healthy and productive growth but restricting eventual size of scions worked upon it, especially fruit trees. M.IX is a very dwarfing root-stock.
See *Malling*

Dyeing

The staining or colouring of plant material by natural or synthetic substances.
See also *Artificially coloured plant material*

Dynamic balance

Refers to various types of contrast or opposing aspects to create interest within the outline of the design which may be symmetrical, asymmetrical, circular, triangular, etc. The visual forces work together as well as against each other to create balance and movement.

E

Easter
Easter Day (the Resurrection) is the first Sunday after the Paschal full moon, ie the full moon on the day after 21 March. Easter falls between 22 March and 25th April.

Easter is a time for decorating the Church with Spring flowers (after Good Friday) and it is also a popular time for weddings.

For flower arrangers and florists alike Easter is therefore a busy time.

Ecology
The study of organisms in relation to their environment and to one another.

Elaeagnaceae   P(4) A4-8 G1
Family of shrubs and small trees covered with brown or silver scales. Includes the Elaegnus (deciduous and evergreen) and Hippophae rham-noides (Sea Buckthorn).

Elaiosome
A seed with oil-producing bodies which attracts ants to assist in dispersal of seeds.

Elements of design
Colour, form, line, space and texture which are the physical characteristics of a flower arrangement design.

Pattern and light can be considered as elements in abstract designing.
See also *Colour, Form, Line, Space* and *Texture*.

Elevation
The profile of a design in terms of height and width without regard to the third dimension.

Also the raising or lifting of plant material to create height (in section or profile).

Elliptic
Leaf shape, widest at the middle, narrowing equally at both ends.

Elongated
Leaves which are long and narrow or slender.

Emarginate
Leaf apex with a notch or depression at the outer end.

Emasculation
Removal of the anthers of a flower in order to prevent self-pollination or the unwanted pollination of plants growing in close proximity.

Embryo
Young plant contained within seed. The embryonic cell divides continuously to produce one or two cotyledons, the radicle and the plumule.

Embryo sac
The large cell structure with a plant ovule that contains the female egg cell.

Empathy/Empathize
One's own emotional or intellectual feelings about a work of art; to see things from another's viewpoint; correctly interpret the attitudes and intentions of others.

Emphasis
An area of the design which needs a degree of dominance and is either a point of heightened interest in an abstract design or a feature which attracts the eye, without necessarily holding it too long. See also *Focal point*

Endocarp
The innermost tissue in a fruit surrounding the seeds and part of the pericarp.
See also *Exocarp*, *Mesocarp* and *Pericarp*

Endodermis
The innermost layer of the root cortex of a plant lying immediately outside the vascular tissue beyond the casparian strip.

Endogenous
Developing or originating within an organism. Lateral roots, which always grow from inside the main root rather than from its surface are said to arise endogenously.

Endoplasmic reticulum
Intracellular membrane system in the cytoplasm in which certain proteins are synthesized. It forms a link between the cell and nuclear membranes.

Endosperm
A tissue within the seed of a flowering plant that surrounds and provides nutrition for the developing embryo. Seeds can be endospermic or non-endospermic; the former increases in size (as in cereals and oil seed crops), the latter disappears as it is absorbed by the embryo.

Entire
Leaf margin without teeth or lobes.

Entomophily
Pollination of a flower by an insect. Such flowers are usually brightly coloured and scented, and often secrete nectar.

Entrelacs
Designs of interlacing bands as applied to knot gardens.

Ephemeral
An annual plant that completes its life cycle in considerably less than one growing season such that a number of generations can occur in a year.

Weeds such as Groundsel are an example. Also used as a term to describe flowers that open for less than a day.

Epicalyx
A series of small sepal-like bracts forming an outer calyx beneath the true calyx in some flowers.

Epicarp
The outer part of the pericarp in fleshy fruits, usually the skin.
Also called *exocarp*

Epicotyl
The seedling stem and part of the embryo on which the first true leaves are formed after hypogeal germination.

Epidermis
The outermost layer of cells covering a plant, overlaid by a cuticle. Its principal function is to protect the plant from injury and to reduce water loss.

Epigeal
Seed germination in which the cotyledons (seed leaves) emerge from the ground and function as true leaves.

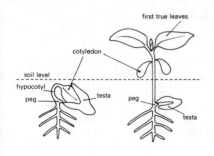

Epigynous
A flower structure where the attachment of the perianth and stamens is above the ovary.

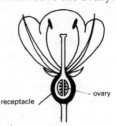

Epiphyte
A plant that grows upon another plant but is not parasitic or rooted in the ground. Mosses and lichens are epiphytes.

Equilateral triangle
Outline or basic shape of an arrangement or design where the base and both sides of the triangle are of equal length.

Equilibrium
A stable condition in which visual forces cancel out one another. In floral art it is the use of features in a design positioned so that the visual attractions would be equally balanced, as well as interest created.

Ericaceae   K4-5 C(4-5) or 4-5
A8-10 $\underline{G}$ (4-5)
A very large family most members of which require soils free from lime. Includes Rhododendron, Arbutus, Erica (Heathers) Kalmia and Pieris.

Ericaceous
Of the family Ericaceae. Also applied to other lime-hating plants.

Espalier
A method of training fruit trees to grow flat as against a wall or on supports to benefit from the sun. The method is also economical in space.

Essential elements

Plants require many elements to manufacture their own starch and sugars and simple chemicals to create proteins, amino acids, vitamins, etc. Carbon is taken from the air, Hydrogen and Oxygen from soil water; *major nutrients* are Nitrogen, Phosphates and Potash; *intermediate nutrients* are Calcium, Magnesium, Sulphur; *trace elements* are Iron, Manganese, Molybdenum, Boron, Zinc and Copper.

Estrade

Topiary pattern of clipped tiers surrounding a trunk.

Etang

Ornamental pond in gardens.

Ethylene

A source of ethylene gas which arises from ripening or rotting fruit – apples in particular. Ethylene can inhibit the opening of flowers which are susceptible – carnations especially.

Etiolation

The abnormal or rapid growth of plants without the production of chlorophyll. Occurs when the plant is grown in darkness or severely reduced light conditions. This produces long, thin and pale shoots, small blanched leaves and a reduced root system.

Etoile

An intersection of straight walks or rides in woodland.

Euphorbiaceae K3-5

or o Co A1-∞ G(2-3)

Small family which includes the Euphorbia and Ricinus. Most of the genus contains latex which exudes when stems are cut.

Evaluation

The critical appraisal of an exhibit or piece of work in order to discover if the requirements of the test have been achieved.

See also *Assessment* and *Judging*

Evanescent

Disappearing soon; transitory.

Evaporation

The process by which a liquid becomes a vapour or gas, eg water evaporates from the surface leaves.

Evergreen

Trees and shrubs, etc, bearing leaves mostly all the year round.

Everlasting flowers

A general term to describe flowers that have been preserved by some means or which do not lose their colour or shape. They are used in dried flower arrangements or framed floral compositions.

Evolution

The gradual changes in organisms that take place under environmental influences.

Ewer

A large, wide-mouthed pitcher or jug, often elaborate if made of pewter or spelter. Can be an attractive container or accessory. Sometimes the bowl section can be porcelain or the ewer made entirely of alabaster.

Exfoliating

Bark peeling off in thin strips or layers (such as Acer griseum).

Exhibit

The accepted term for a flower arrangement or design in competitive or exhibition work. It is plant material with or without accessories which has to conform to the rules of the show schedule in respect of space allowed, and to other conditions specified. It has superseded the word 'arrangement'.

Expressionism

A movement in modern art where artists were concerned with emotional responses to subjects rather than actual representation. A private, personal and modern concept representing feelings of anger, humility, etc, in distorted shapes and colours not matched to reality. See also *Impressionism*

Expressive abstract   (figurative)

A design concept where a subject theme is interpreted in abstract terms and construction. The design implies, it does not represent or depict reality, only the arranger's feelings about the subject. Plant material has to predominate and if fresh, must be in water or water-retaining material. Category no longer differentiated in Abstract classes.

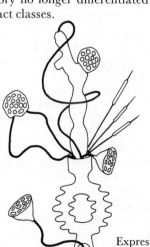

Exserted

Stamens projecting beyond the Corolla.

Exstipulate

Without stipules.

Extended legs

A form of wiring to lengthen the stem of a flower if it is too short. A previously wired flower (for support) is mounted with a single leg mount both of which are then taped.
See also *Single-leg mount*

External wiring

A previously taped wire is inserted into the base of the flower or calyx and is twisted down the stem and between leaf nodes (if applicable).

Extrorse

Turned or opening outwards; anthers which open to shed pollen on the face away from the axis of the flowers.

Exude

To secrete liquid from pores or from a cut surface such as sap from trees.

Expressive Abstract 'Echoes'   59

F

F₁, hybrids

First filial generation (filial = resembling). The seed produced by arranged cross-fertilization from true-breeding parent plants. F_1 plants are identical in every respect, ie flower size, colour and flowering period. Seeds from F_1 plants do not perpetuate these characteristics.

F₂

Second filial generation arising from crosses between individuals of the F_1 generation.

Facing arrangement

An arrangement of flowers and foliage, etc, which is looked at from one direction only, namely from the front. It is now more a florist's concept since the flower arranger's movement is attempting to have the term replaced by other descriptions.

Falcate

Leaf shaped like a sickle (curved sideways).

Falls

The outer spreading or recurved perianth segments of an Iris.

False fruit

A fruit such as the apple, strawberry or hop that includes material other than the ripe ovary.

False legs

The addition of a mount wire to replace or extend a natural stem of a flower.

False rings

Rings in timber which appear to be annual rings but which are not complete. They are caused by severe frost, other damage or defoliation.

Family

A 'fourth order' category in the classification of plants in the Plant Kingdom. Consists of related genera determined by the structure of the flower which is identical within a family.

A family is a natural order and names end in -aceae, or, -ae.

Farinose

Covered with a white mealy substance as with some primulas and auriculas.

Fasciated

Abnormal flattening of stems due to

failure of lateral branches to separate from main stem. Some interesting and useful forms of plant material are produced by this abnormality.

Fascicle
A bundle or cluster of branches, leaves, etc.

Fastigiate
Having erect branches which are close together and often appear to create a single column with the trunk.

Fauvism
Essentially a two-dimensional art; painting where light and shadow are believed equally luminous, resulting in contrasting hues rather than tones. Pure, brilliant colours were a feature. Lasted for only two years 1905-1907 with Matisse being the central figure.

Feathering
Taking separate petals from a carnation and wiring two or three together to make a smaller unit for a Corsage, Bouquet or Victorian Posy.

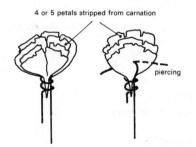
4 or 5 petals stripped from carnation

piercing

Feathers
Any of the light, flat structures constituting the plumage of birds. Feathers may be used in competitive work, provided that accessories are permitted. Feathers can help to reinforce a theme in Oriental and Period work.

Featuring
To include a component in an exhibit as specifically required in a show schedule; to give a component greater emphasis than if it was integrated or incorporated.
See also *Incorporate, integrate*

Female flower
A flower having an ovary but no fertile stamens.

Ferme ornée
'Ornamental farm', where a combination of farm and garden formed a type of Landscape gardening. A feature is the ornamentation of hedgerows by planting shrubs and climbers within and a wide herbaceous border in front. Idea described by Stephen Switzer in 1715 and first introduced by the Hon Charles Hamilton (1704-1786) at Painshill, Surrey.

Fern
A pteridophyte belonging to the order Filicales. Ferns have spirally arranged leaves, called fronds, which are often pinnately compound. Fern spores are carried on the under side (abaxial) surface of the fronds in structures (sori).

Fernery
Glasshouses built in Victorian times to accommodate the exotic ferns collected in Wardian cases and sent to England by plant hunters from 1833 onwards. Also refers to an outdoor group of ferns.

Ferruginous
Rust coloured.

Fertile

Organisms which produce offspring, or reproductive organs which produce viable gametes or are capable of producing spores, pollen, seeds or fruit.

Fertilization

The process whereby a male gamete and a female gamete fuse to make a zygote.
See also *Self-fertilization* and *Cross-fertilization*

Fertilizer

Material added to soils to provide nutrients for plant growth. Can be in liquid or powder form, or slow-release granules which dissipate over a period of time. Often a balanced NPK formula, (Nitrogen, Phosphorus, Potassium) with trace elements formulated for the special needs of plants. Can also be organic or inorganic.

Fibre

An elongated plant cell whose walls are extensively thickened with lignin. Fibres are in the vascular tissue, usually in the xylem and some species are of importance commercially, eg Flax.

Fibrous roots

System consisting of a tuft of adventitious roots of more or less

equal diameter, originating at the stem base and bearing smaller lateral roots. See also *Tap roots*

Figurine

Small, carved or moulded statuette, either a single figure or group of figures on a base, or part of the body (human or animal) which may be incorporated into a container or used separately as an accessory.

Filament

The stalk of the stamen bearing the anther. Consists mainly of conducting tissue attaching the anther to the receptacle.

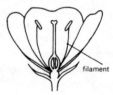

Filicales

An order of the Class Filicopsida in the Division Pteridophyta to which all typical ferns belong. See also *Fern*

Filler material

The use of transitional forms of plant material to complete the design or to hide mechanics. If used too much it can weaken a bold impact or mask other flower forms.

Filiform

Having the form of a thread.

Fimbriate

Leaf or petal margins having fringed edge.

Fir
Description of a number of coniferous evergreen trees of the genus Abies (Pine family).

Fission
Splitting into two or more parts. A form of asexual reproduction in a unicellular plant, involving a division into two or more equal parts that develop into new cells.

Flaccid
Plant tissue that has become softer than normal because a loss of water has caused the cytoplasm to shrink.

Fleshy
Thick and pulpy organs such as fruit and leaves, which are often juicy.

Flexuous
Sinuous, full of bends and curves.

Floccose
Covered with woolly hairs.

Flora
(1) Plants collectively; especially the plants of a given place or time; a descriptive list of such plants including an identification key.
(2) Roman goddess of flowers.

Floral art
An alternative expression for flower arranging – a design decorated with, or consisting of, flowers (but also to include foliage, etc) and embracing the craft aspects associated with it, as well as Modern and Abstract work.

Floral clock
A clock face planted in carpet bedding below which was a mechanism for controlling the hands which could also be ornamentally planted. Usually found in public parks from 1910 onwards, especially at seaside resorts.

Floral diagram
A diagram showing the position and number of all the parts of a flower in transverse cross-section.

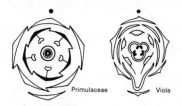

Primulaceae   Viola

Floral envelope
The part of the flower that surrounds the stamens and pistil, together with the calyx and corolla, ie the perianth.

Floral foam
A synthetic material produced in two forms. One is for 'dry' arrangements the other can be soaked and has water retaining properties. Now available in rounds, blocks, large spheres, etc, and also shaped for funeral work (hearts, crosses, etc) inserted in plastic trays. For large exhibits the foam can be covered with wire mesh (chicken wire) to give added support for strong stems and to prevent the floral foam from disintegrating. The 'dry' form is usually brown in colour, the wet form green.

Floral formula
Method of compressing information for identifying family of plants.
K = calyx (number of sepals)
C = corolla (number of petals)
A = the androecium (number of stamens), (the male parts of the flower)

G = the gynoecium (number of carpels), (the female parts of the flower)

eg Primulaceae K(5) C(5) A5 $\underline{G}$(5)

K(5) = 5 sepals
C(5) = 5 petals } joined together

A5 = 5 stamens

$\underline{G}$(5) = 5 pistils with superior ovary (joined together)

$\underline{G}$ means that the pistil has a superior ovary

$\bar{G}$ means that the pistil has an inferior ovary

G means that both inferior and superior ovaries may be present.

The figures indicate the number of parts of which it is composed. If the figures are in brackets then all parts are joined together and cannot be separated without tearing.

Other symbols are:

P = perianth

∞ numerous or indefinite

+ between figures to show the separation of the parts into two or more layers or whorls

♂ = male

♀ = female

☿ = hermaphrodite

⊕ = actinomorphic

1|1 = zygomorphic

Florescence

The condition, time or period of blossoming.

Floret

(1) A small flower.

(2) One of many making up the head of a composite flower, further identified as disk-floret; the central part and ray floret which is the flower at the outer edge of the inflorescence.

(3) *Tubular* where all the petals are the same size forming a tube.

(4) *Ligulate* where one petal is larger than the others and is strap-shaped.

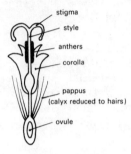

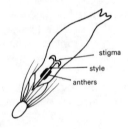

Floribunda

Any type of cultivated hybrid rose whose flowers grow in clusters or sprays; named as such in the 1950s. New classification from 1971 as 'cluster-flowered roses'.

Floriferous

Bearing or capable of bearing many flowers.

Florilegium

A lavishly illustrated book on a collection of flowers.

Florist

The historical term for one who cultivated flowers not one who offers them for sale. Societies of Florists were established towards the middle of 17th century, those in Norwich and London being the earliest. Specialist florist flowers include Polyanthus, Pink, Auricula, Tulip, etc.

Nowadays, the term for one who is professionally trained and works in, or owns, a business selling flowers and sundries and is skilled in making-up flowers for weddings or funeral tributes, etc.

Floristics

A branch of Botany concerned with the statistics of a plant species in a particular area, viz types, numbers and distribution.

Flower

(1) The reproductive part of an angiosperm – flowers are modified special shoots. They are made up of sepals and petals, stamens and carpels.
See also *Perianth*, *Corolla* and *Calyx*
(2) Any single flower head (eg daffodil or dahlia) or group of heads springing from a single stem (eg delphinium, gladiolus, etc).

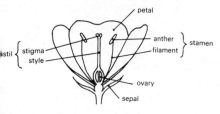

Flower ball

An appropriate arrangement for a child bridesmaid made up with mixed flowers and small foliage and constructed in a spherical shape with a ribbon carrying handle and bows. It is a popular and easy way for small children to carry flowers and can be tied to the wrist to prevent mishap. When completed it is the size of a

large orange. Sometimes called a *pomander*. See definition of this term.

Flower festivals

The organization and design of exhibits for a church or historic house, etc, either to commemorate an occasion or to raise money for a charity. They can range from a small village church to those at Westminster Abbey organized by NAFAS. Sometimes a set theme portrays the occasion.

Flower picks

A substitute for wiring stems made either of wood or metal. The former is rather like a cocktail stick whereas the wire pick is sharp at one end and has a fine wire on the other which is wound around the flower stem. In both types the sharp ends are stabbed into the base.

Flower preservative
Various chemicals, commercially available in sachet form, for adding to the water in floral arrangements to keep it germ free and to act as a feed for the cut flowers.

Flower press
A construction for pressing flowers, comprising two square outer wooden boards with bolts at each corner and wing-nuts for tightening screws. The interleaves of card spacers accommodate the plant material for pressing.

Fluorescent light
Light emitted from tubes in which an electrical gas discharge is maintained causing the mercury vapour to emit ultraviolet radiation and the phosphor coating to fluoresce. The (white) tube always imparts a slight blue cast which turns red colours to muddy brown and yellows slightly green. Acid yellows and greens benefit, blues and violets become intense. Glaucous foliage is enhanced and whites tend to stay clean.

Flush
A period of fresh growth of leaves shoots or flowers.

Fluted
The bole of a tree with the bark or shape having rounded grooves running vertically.

Focal hold
See *Focal point*

Focal point
Central point of attention or interest in an arrangement or design (NOT actual central point). In traditional designs it is normally created by use of blooms of larger size or stronger colour, placed under the tip of the tallest placement and where the eye rests within the design.

Foliaceous
Leaf-like.

Foliage
The leaves of a plant collectively and the sprays of leaves used in flower decoration or exhibition work.

Foliage corsage
Corsage designed and made up entirely of foliage in different forms, textures, sizes and colours.

Foliar feeding
Feeding plants through the leaves by spraying with a fine mist which contains soluble nutrients. Micronutrients applied in this way can reach the sap stream within one hour of application. It is a good way to feed plants in dry weather.

Follicle
A dry dehiscent fruit from a single

carpel that when ripe splits along one side to release its seeds.

Folly
Sham buildings built at the whim of an owner to deceive or catch the eye. Constructed in all shapes and forms, they are very personal expressions, giving visual interest to a park landscape. A feature of 18th century fashion in park and large garden design.

Font
Usually a carved stone base mounted on a plinth within which is contained a bowl of baptismal water. The font usually has a wooden top or ornate canopy. It is often decorated with flowers at Easter and Christmas, but for Christenings the decorations must not impede the baptism ceremony.

Forcing
The means of advancing the opening of flowers by giving extra warmth. Stems of flowering shrubs can be induced to flower early in the Spring by immersing them in warm water and keeping in warm conditions.

Forecourt
An historic architectural feature in garden design generally at the front of the mansion.

Form
(1) The overall picture of the design, ie what form or pattern it will take and which style or intent is created.
(2) The shape of something and/or the arrangement of its parts; usually regarded as three dimensional, solid or volumetric. In analysis of forms of plant material it is possible to generalize and classify into three shapes, viz points, lines and the material in between, known as *transitional shapes*.
(3) Form not only includes shape but also other aspects such as size, texture, colour, tone and visual movement.

Formal
A bouquet, buttonhole or arrangement suitable for the occasion and/or ceremony.

Formal posy
A freely arranged design with a circular outline and a gently domed profile. Natural flower material on its own or wired stems either using one type of flower, or several, with one or more colours.

Foundation work (basing, blocking)
The massing of flowers on a prepared funeral tribute base, the stems of which have been shortened or removed. They are mounted appropriately and pinned to the frame to give a massed fabric-like effect, with maximum coverage: at the same time it should preserve the shape of the base outline.

Fountain
A classical garden feature which owes its origins to the Romans. Fountains were constructed in most Renaiss-

ance gardens and were their most important single feature. They are still popular in parks today.

Frame (cold frame)
Structure forming low support for lights and used for the frost protection of low growing plants until hardened off. See also *Lights*

Free-central
Type of placentation in which the ovules are borne on a central stem growing from the base of the ovary, which is one-celled without any inner walls, or where the ovules are rudimentary. See also *Placenta*

Free-form (free style)
Modern designs, free from geometric form or style, and created outside the basic traditional outlines. Uses nature's infinite variations of form to dictate the design. The predomin-ance of plant material is organized in a conventional manner radiating from a given point. It is not Abstract work.

Free-standing
Exhibits that must be on a base, plinth or pedestal without any other means of support. In certain show classes they are meant to be viewed from all sides.

Fresh plant material
Naturally growing or cultivated flowers and foliage which have been

cut from a living plant and condi-tioned so that cut stems last as long as possible in water and/or water-retaining material.

In competitive work all cut stems MUST be in water or water-retaining material. Exceptions to this rule are fruit, vegetables, succulents, cacti, air plants, moss, lichen and natural grass turf.

Friable
Soil structure that is easily broken up and workable – indicating the good loose condition of the soil.

Frit
Finely-ground silicates with trace elements incorporated.

Frog
A plastic, four-pronged holder to secure floral foam to the bowl of a container. It is affixed with adhesive plasticine for added security. An integral part of some plastic containers.

Frond
The compound (pinnate or bi-pinnate) leaf of a fern; the leaf of a palm or cycad; the thallus of a seaweed or lichen.

Frottage
Taking an impression from a raised or textured surface by covering with a sheet of paper and rubbing it with charcoal or another soft drawing material. Often incorporated into

Surrealist collages. Technique of brass-rubbing in churches today.

Fruit

Structure formed from the ovary after the ovules have been fertilized. The function of the fruit is both to protect the seeds and assist in their dispersal.

In competitive floral art, fruit embraces all edible and inedible forms, including berries, seedheads, cones, nuts, fungi and also vegetables. Grasses, cereals, reeds, rushes and catkins may be used as fruit at any stage of their development.

Funeral spray

A design which can be made up in moss on a wire frame, in floral foam on a wood board, pad or other foundation. Flower material, natural or not, with or without foliage and wired only if necessary is arranged with a suitable outline, with some elevation in profile and a focal point.

Funeral work

An important aspect of the floristry profession; created in many styles and a variety of tributes ranging from a simple bunch of flowers from a grandchild to the most extravagant thematic design for a celebrity.

Funeral work is divided into foundation work and loose work.
See also *Foundation work* and *Loose work*

Fungicide

Chemical agents which kill or prevent development of fungi spores.

Fungus

Any simple plant of the Fungi Division lacking chlorophyll, leaves, true stems and roots. Reproduces by spores and lives as a parasite or saprophytically by making use of rotting organic material.
See also *Bracket-fungus*

Funicle

The stalk that attaches an ovule to the placenta in the ovary of a flowering plant.

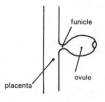

Fusiform

Elongated and tapering at both ends – spindle shaped.

Futurism

Expression introduced by the poet Marinetti in 1909. The most important concept was simultaneously showing overlapping planes in sequence to represent motion. Also based on the idea that no object, whether moving or stationary is seen in isolation. Marcel Duchamp's (1887-1968) 'Nude descending a Staircase' II (1911-1912) is a famous example.

G

G
The symbol for gynoecium (female parts) of a flower in the floral formula. See also *Flower structure*

Gall
Abnormal swelling of plant tissues in response to irritation caused by insects, fungi or bacteria.

Gametes
Reproductive cells that fuse with another gamete of the opposite sex to form a zygote. Gametes are formed by meiosis. They are haploid (contain half the normal number of chromosomes). Also called a *sex cell*.

Gamopetalous
A flower having the petals joined, or partly so, and the corolla thus becomes a tube.

Garden plant material
Natural and cultivated flowers and foliage, etc, which can be grown outside in the British Isles without complete overhead protection at all times.

Garland
Plant material assembled into an elongated and flexible design for draping in a decorative way. It does not have a visible background. It has its origins in ancient history especially Greek and Roman.

Gate
A functional and/or decorative feature of European gardens. The earliest designs were wooden but later on in the 17th century Jean Tijon who came to England in 1689 produced designs which have not been surpassed (Hampton Court). Gates and pillars became less prominent in the 18th century. Development in the 19th and 20th centuries produced a less decorative but more functional boundary entrance to an estate. Painted in flamboyant fashion in the 1700s (bright green or blue and heavily gilded), they are nowadays generally painted black with some features picked out in gold.

Gatehouse
A functional and decorative building

at the entrance to a country mansion constructed as either a single building pierced by a gateway or twin or single lodges beside the gates, sometimes linked with a single arch. Many fine examples of varying architectural styles are still to be seen, (Stanway House, Glos. Charlcote, Warwicks).

Gates of Heaven
A massed funeral tribute design with an archway over a base. A wire cross surmounts the arch and wire gates are left ajar, neither of which are mossed nor covered with flowers but are usually painted black or gold.

Gazebo
A structure, either an elevated room placed on a natural vantage point or the main room on the first floor of a garden building designed to give an elevated outlook. Now applied to domed ironwork or fibre glass, constructed as a focal point without necessarily being elevated.

Gazon coupé
Shapes cut from turf and filled with coloured gravel to form a pattern.

Gene
A unit of inheritance – a length of DNA in a chromosome that codes a particular character of the cell. It exists in different forms called *alleles*. See also *Chromosome*

Generation
Set of individuals of roughly equal age or stage of development. The parents are of one generation, the progeny (offspring) are the next.

Genetics
The study of heredity and variations in organisms.

Genus
A category used in classification of plants that consists of a number of closely related species. The name of the genus is the first in a Latin binomial nomenclature.
See also *Binomial nomenclature*
Anemone (*genus*), hupehensis (*species*), 'superba' (*variety*)

Geometric style
An arrangement with a definite geometric form which can be predominantly mass or line but which should have a recognisable outline. This can be crescent, Hogarth curve, vertical, diagonal, triangular, 'L' shape, etc.

Geotropism
The curving growth of a stem in response to the stimulus of gravity. Plant stems which grow upwards

71

show negative tropism, roots growing downwards show positive tropism.

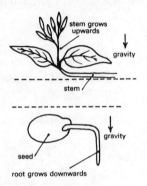

stem grows upwards

gravity

stem

gravity

seed

root grows downwards

Geraniaceae   K5 C5 A5-10 G̲5
Small family includes the Erodium, Pelargonium and Geranium.

Germination
Emergence of root from seed coat denoting development of plant. The first stage in the growth of a seed into a seedling. Normally occurs only under certain conditions of temperature, moisture and oxygen.

Some seeds need special conditions before germination such as light, scarification, chipping or stratification. See also *Epigeal* and *Hypogeal*

Gestalt
A German term for 'form, figure, fashion, manner and shape' used in aesthetics. The concept is that 'the whole is greater than the sum of its parts' and it is believed better to understand and analyse the whole rather than acquire many separate elements and attempt a synthesis.

Gibberellin
A group of plant growth substances chemically related to gibberellic acid.

They promote shoot elongation and are useful in promoting seed germination and releasing buds from dormancy.

Gift wrap
Method of making up a presentation of flowers and foliage, attractively arranged, with stems tied together placed in a cellophane-faced bag and finished with a decorative bow of ribbon. Stems of cut materials are covered to finish off the gift wrap and also to reduce dehydration and damage. Also a method of presentation for pot plants.

Glabrous
Without hairs or similar growth; smooth.

Gland
A cell or group of cells or organ that synthesizes and secretes a particular substance.

Glaucous
Covered with a waxy or bluish-green bloom.

Glittering
The use of small flakes of highly reflective and decorative material which are glued on to plant material etc, to give it a festive look (at Christmas). It comes under the category of 'artificially coloured plant material'.

Globose
Spherical or nearly so.

Glucose
In the form of dextrose a major energy source for plants. It is a

product of photosynthesis $C_6H_{12}O_6$. See also *Starch*

Glue gun

An electrically heated means of dissolving solid glue-sticks and directing glue to a fine point. Useful for securing made-up dried plant material and delicate floristry work.

Glycerine

Another name for glycerol, a colourless, sweet-tasting, syrup-like liquid which is a by-product of soap manufacture. Used in diluted form for preserving plant material especially foliage. Anti-freeze can be used as an alternative.

Golden section

A proportion (known also as the golden mean) used for centuries by artists in the composition of paintings. It relates to a ratio of approximately 5:8 and is regularly found in nature. Established by Euclid and written up by Pacioli in Davina Proportione and illustrated by Leonardo da Vinci.

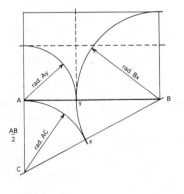

Gourd

Fruit of certain members of the melon family having colourful and textured skins and being decorative for some appropriate designs.

Grading

(1) The selection of flowers into categories for sale at a market and a process of removing sub-standard or damaged blooms.
(2) The selection of various sizes of plant material in order to preserve a good scale relationship. It is a characteristic of traditional designs where large flowers in the centre of the design give way to smaller, graded, sizes towards the edges.

Graft

To join together, by artificial means, parts from two different plants. There are many types of grafting, viz whip and tongue, saddle, splice, etc. A graft is the union of the scion (the desired variety) with the rootstock (a common or wild species). The stock supplies the scion with water and mineral salts and is a means of regulating the growth of trees by grafting on to dwarfing rootstock.

Gramineae   P0 A1-6 G1

Large family of the grasses divided into twelve tribes. Includes the Bamboos.

Grasses

Monocotyledons of the Gramineae family containing all the cultivated cereals. In competitive work grasses may be used either as flowers or fruit, whatever their stage of development.

Green

A secondary colour from the mixture

of blue and yellow pigments. Symbolic of youth and cool fertile growth. It induces tranquillity and produces less eye strain than any other colour.

Zodiac: Taurus

Heraldry: Vert   Youth and fertility
   effect under tungsten light: greyish-green
   effect under white fluorescent light: green

Opt app	Psycho eff	Symb interp
quiet	soothing	hope
passive	relaxing	peace
simple	rejuvenation	nature
bluer– more moist	preservation	joy
more yellow		youth
–warmer	healing	
cool	selfishness	Spring
fresh		faith
tranquil		envy
		sea
		fecundity
		sympathy
		Ireland
		Venus

Greenhouse

Structure of framework housing glass, in many shapes and sizes and with several types of materials for the framework. Can be heated or un-heated. Used for protecting and growing all types of plants. Some designed for special use, eg Alpine Houses.

In the commercial world the structure is referred to as *glasshouse*.

Greenhouse effect

The effect within a greenhouse in which solar radiation passes through the glass and is absorbed in the floor, earth and contents and in turn re-emits the energy as infra-red radiation. Since this cannot escape through the glass temperature within rises.

Greening

In funeral wreath work, the covering or edging of the mossed frame with small pieces of evergreen (usually conifers) with single or double-leg mounting placed into the moss as appropriate for the design.

Grey

An achromatic colour (ie devoid of chroma) which is any tint or shade between black and white. Greys are the shadows and the veiling mists of nature. All colours can be used with grey which, as a neutral, matches them without visual conflict.

Zodiac: Aquarius   *Heraldry*: not in use

Opt app	Psycho eff	Symb interp
ghostly	characterless	old age
sterile	neutralising	twilight
neutral	blending	tribulation
light or dark		fear
according to	restrained	
tone	resignation	poverty
cool/cold		repression
mists		neutrality
		frugality
		dignity
		storm
		clouds
		(dark)
		shadows

Grille
Vertical iron rods, sometimes elaborately wrought to make fences or gates.

Grooming
The care of the fabrics and plant material in an exhibit so that blemishes on flowers or leaves are removed and creases ironed out of drapes, etc. Also the removal of debris or particles of dirt, etc, from the exhibit to make it an immaculate presentation.

Grotto
A natural or artificial imitation of a cave, becoming part of the English landscape garden in the 18th century. A feature of Italian Renaissance gardens.

Ground-cover
The practice of planting large areas with low-growing plants which will merge and suppress weeds. They can be either low-growing shrubs, conifers or perennials. A style of gardening which is gaining in popularity.

Grouping
The making-up of flowers and foliage of a particular colour in funeral work to form a group on any shaped base in order to give a focal point and interest to the overall design.

Grove
A grouping of trees, growing naturally or planted in formation and usually of the same species.

Growing point
The leading part of a shoot or branch from which a tree or shrub continues to grow.

Growth
An increase in the dry weight (or volume) of a plant through cell division and cell enlargement.

Growth ring
A ring that can be seen in the cross section of a tree trunk representing the xylem formed in one year. The age of a tree can be determined by counting the (annual) growth rings.

Growth substances
Certain chemicals which promote growth and plant development and which are synthesized to emulate naturally occurring hormones. They are not fertilizers.
   Some substances can promote root growth and others can control or retard growth.

Guard cell
See *Stoma*

Gum
Any of various sticky substances that exude from certain plants which are produced by the young xylem vessels. The gum hardens on exposure to air providing a temporary protective seal whilst healing the wound.

Guttation
The process whereby sap or water exudes through hydathodes (ends of veins of glands at leaf margins), eg Fuchsia.

Gymnospermae
A subdivision of the spermatophyta containing the conifers and related species.
   The gametes are contained in male and female cones. The ovules are borne naked.

Gynoecium

The female sex organs (carpels) of a flower represented by the letter G in floral formulae and consisting of one or more pistils. See also *Pistil*

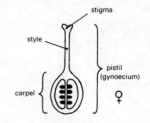

H

Habit
The general appearance of a plant, method of growth, type of existence or conditions controlling form.

Habitat
The natural home of a plant characterized by the physical environment or the dominant plant types which abound.

Ha-ha
A sunken fence formed by excavating a deep ditch with a masonry retaining wall built on the house side to prevent animals leaping or climbing into the park or garden. The object was to create an uninterrupted view and visual continuity from lawn to pasture. French in origin in the 17th century.

Half head-dress
A head-dress for either a bride or adult bridesmaid made up of either mixed flowers and foliage or flowers of one kind and worn across the top of the head.

Halophyte
A plant adapted to living in salty conditions.

Hamamelidaceae   K(4-5) C4-5
   or o A4-5 G̲(2)
A family of trees and shrubs which includes Corylopsis, Fothergilla,
Hamamelis (Witch Hazel), Liquidambar and Parrotia.

Hanging basket
A galvanized wire hemispherical construction (with link chains for suspension) which is lined with moss and filled with compost in which flowering plants are planted for multicolour display, generally in the summer months. It is possible to have baskets planted for different seasons in the year, either for herbs or all one type of plant, eg fuchsia.
    There are also plastic forms of hanging basket available in different sizes and colours.

Hanging-wood
A wood which either crowns a hill or which 'hangs' on the side of it, a feature of the English landscape garden.

Haploid
A nucleus, cell or organism with a single set of unpaired chromosomes. See also *Diploid*

Haptotropism
Also called thigmotropism – the directional growth of a plant in response to the stimulus of touch.

Hardboard
Fairly thin stiff sheeting made of sawdust and woodchip compressed

and bound together with resin or similar adhesive under heat and pressure. One side is smooth and the reverse is textured. It is used for construction of backgrounds and as a backing for pictures. See also *Pegboard*

Harden-off
To gradually accustom young plants to tolerate more rigorous growing conditions, eg in the sequence greenhouse – to cold frame – to outside (without overhead protection) and finally to planted positions.

Harmony
Order of parts to their whole or to one another; regarded as the eventual outcome when all the principles and elements of design are used well and when all components are related in appearance with a similar style throughout the design.

Hastate
Simple leaf shape having a pointed tip with two outward-pointing lobes at the base.

Haulm
The stems and foliage of some plants such as Sweet Peas, grasses, potatoes, etc.

Head
(1) The cluster of fruit or flowers crowded at the end of a common peduncle (stalk), eg Hydrangea.

(2) The branching system of a standard or half-standard tree.

Head-dress
A design of flowers to be worn in the hair by a bride and adult and child bridesmaids. May be made entirely of one type of flower or mixed.
See also *Back-spray head-dress, Half head-dress, Coronet, Cluster head-dress* and *Tiara*

Heart
Shape of funeral tribute, in various sizes, either open-frame or cushion type. The cushion type has a flat base with a raised lid to give convex shape to the top part. The heart shape is also available in water-retaining material within a plastic base.

Heartwood
The wood at the centre of a tree trunk or branch consisting of dead xylem cells strengthened with lignin and giving structural support. It is often darker in colour and is unable to conduct sap.

Hedge
A boundary of trees or shrubs to protect a garden from intruders and offer some protection from the wind. Hedges vary from very tall species of laurel, etc, to dwarf Box (Buxus)

shaped and trimmed to create patterns for knot gardens, to the flowering hedges that are popular today.

Heel
A portion of older tissue at the base of a young shoot which has been torn from the parent.
See also *Stem cutting, heel*

heel

Heel-in
To temporarily bury rooted shrubs or plants into soil or other medium so as to prevent drying out if the plants cannot be planted out immediately after purchase due to adverse weather conditions.

Herb
(1) A seed-bearing plant whose aerial parts do not remain above ground at the end of the growing season or (2) any of the usually aromatic plants used in cookery or medicine such as parsley, thyme, rue, rosemary, etc.

Herbaceous border
A border or flower bed that contains perennial plants rather than annuals or woody plants and which is usually set against a wall or hedge. Popularized by Gertrude Jekyll towards the end of the 19th century.
See also *Herbaceous plant* and *Mixed border*

Herbaceous plant (perennial)
A plant whose aerial parts die down each winter, the underground parts remaining alive, shooting up again each Spring and living for more than two years. See also *Woody perennial*

Herbarium
Room or building to house a classified collection of botanical specimens for reference and identification purposes.

Heredity
The transmission, from one generation to the next, of those genetic factors that determine individual characteristics between parents and offspring.

Hermaphrodite (bisexual)
A plant whose flowers contain both male organs (stamens) and female organs (carpels). The usual arrangement in the majority of flowering plants.

Heterozygous
An organism that has two different alleles controlling a particular features.
    The F_1 generation is heterozygous.

High-key
An arrangement, picture or photograph having a predominance of light grey tones or light colours.
See also *Low key*

Hilum
A scar on the seed coat of a plant marking the point at which the seed was attached to the fruit wall by the funicle.

Hip (or hep)
The fleshy indehiscent fruit of a rose.

Some hips are very decorative for flower arranging and preserve quite well if varnished.

Hirsute
Covered with long but not stiff hairs.

Hispid
Covered with stiff erect hairs.

Hogarth curve
Attributed to William Hogarth (1697-1764), English painter and engraver. A geometric style/shape of flower arrangement in the form of an 'S'-shaped line (often referred to as a lazy 'S'). It can be either vertical, or less commonly, horizontal in placement.

Homogamy
The condition in a flower in which the male and female reproductive organs mature at the same time thus allowing self-fertilization.

Homologous
Having a related or similar structure.

Homozygous
An organism having two identical alleles controlling a particular feature which may be either dominant or recessive.

Honey fungus (Armillaria mellea)
A parasite on the roots of trees and shrubs producing long, black, thin 'bootlace' underground strands which can kill roots by drawing nourishment from them. The fungus-shaped mushrooms can be seen at the base of dead or dying trees.

Honey guide
The pattern of lines or spots on the petals of certain flowers, the object of which is to guide insects to the nectary.

Hooded
Flowers whose petal tips are curved inwards or which have a hood as part of the petal formation eg Sweet Pea, Aconitum (Monkshood).

Hook
A modified part of the stem used by certain plants for climbing; hooks may be found on any part of the stem and sometimes on leaf petioles.

Hook method
A form of internal wiring where the tip is fashioned into a small hook in order to catch the internal central part of the flower to prevent the wire from slipping right through. Unsuitable wiring method for flowers with an open centre.

Horizontal
Parallel to the plane of the horizon and flat. An axis for a 'line' design where the emphasis is low in profile.

Hormone
A chemical substance as an organic compound produced by a plant (in very small amounts) and essential for growth. There are five main groups: auxins, gibberellins, ethene, abscisic acid and cytokinins.

Hormone rooting medium
Synthetic powder or liquid used to promote rooting of cuttings and available in various strengths.

Hose-in-hose
An arrangement of some of the flowers of the primrose and Polyanthus family where the flowers grow in pairs within each other. See also *Jack-in-the-Green*

Hostess bouquet
Flowers and foliage arranged in the hand and tied. It should be an all-round assembly in a well defined shape of a loose open cone. The objective is to allow the bouquet to be placed in a vase without further arrangement.

Hue
Colour at full spectrum strength. The attribute (name) which denotes whether a colour is Red, Yellow, Orange, Violet, etc.

Humidity
The amount of water vapour in the atmosphere measured in percentage terms. Part of the conditions required for some plants of tropical origin and for growth of stem cuttings taken from shrubs, etc.

Humus
Dark-coloured amorphous material that constitutes the organic component of soil. It is formed by the decomposition of plant and animal remains and manures. Being a colloid it holds water. It enhances soil fertility and improves workability.

Hyaline
Thin and translucent.

Hybrid
The offspring from a plant which results from the cross-fertilization of two different species, sub-species, varieties or strains. It is indicated by a multiplication sign eg Spiraea x bumalda 'Anthony Waterer'.

Hybridization
The technique of selecting appropriate plants and cross-breeding to produce new crosses or to 'clean up' stock to re-establish original hybrids.

Hydathode
A pore, in the epidermis of leaves in certain plants, enabling it to secrete water under conditions of excess humidity when transpiration is inhibited. See also *Guttation*

Hydrophyte
A plant that lives either in very wet soil, partially submerged, or completely under water, eg Water Lilies.

Hydroponics
A technique for growing certain crop plants in culture solutions rather than soil. The nutrients are fed to the roots by means of an aerated solution.

Hydrotropism
The growth of a plant in response to

water, eg the roots search out water in the soil.

Hygroscopic
Absorbing water readily as, for example, moisture from atmosphere.

Hypericaceae   K4-5 C4-5
   A ∞ G̲(3-5)
A small family consisting of mainly sp. of Hypericum (St John's Wort).

Hypocotyl
The stem beneath the stalks of cotyledons (seed leaves) but directly above the young root of an embryo plant.

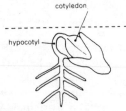

Hypodermis
The outermost layer of cells in a plant lying immediately below the epidermis, in the leaves, stems and roots.

Hypogeal
Seed germination in which the cotyledons (seed leaves) remain below ground, such as runner bean. See also *Epigeal*

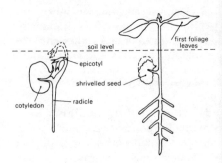

Hypogynous
When the attachment of the perianth and stamens grow from the base of the gynoecium giving a superior ovary.

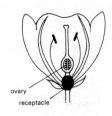

I

IAA
Indole acetic acid, the most common auxin which is produced in the shoot apex. See also *Auxin*

Ice-house
Usually built in a well-drained and cool part of the garden, constructed of brick or stone, covered with clay and then soil. Capable of storing winter ice for up to two years. Popular in 18th and 19th century. Some were elaborate Gothic or Classical structures.

Ikebana
The Japanese word for flower-arrangements and means 'living flowers'. It is a contemplative yet scientific style of arrangement and there are many schools most of which did not come into existence until the end of the 15th century. The earliest school is Ikenobu AD 700. Ikebana is non-competitive.

Imbibition
The process in which water is taken up by a dry seed before it germinates. Along with osmosis this is responsible for the growth of plant cells.

Imbricate
Leaves, scales, overlapping each other.

Immune
Plants which by their nature are unaffected by certain pests or diseases.

Imparipinnate
Pinnate leaves having a terminal unpaired leaflet. See also *Pinnate*

Impermeable
Membranes which do not allow the movement of substances from one side through to the other.

Impressed
Sunken – as veins in leaves.

Impressionism
A movement which originated in France in the 1870s, the object being to achieve a high degree of naturalism through detailed analysis and depiction of light on a surface by use of key colours and disconnected brush strokes. In floral art it is the communication of inner feelings produced by seeing a place, person or

object, ie representation of vision into form.

Inbreeding
To breed with an identical or genetically similar individual plant and so reduce a variation of the species.

Incised
A leaf shape, usually serrated, where the blade is sharply and deeply divided, usually irregularly (and toothed).

Included
Stamens concealed within the corolla or perianth.

Incompatible
Two plants which cannot breed with each other; a mechanism which prevents self fertilization.

Incomplete dominance
The condition that arises when neither allele controlling characteristics is dominant thus producing partial influence from both.

Incorporate
To include; usually stated as an instruction for a component to be used in a class in a show schedule. It is obligatory to use the object stated within the exhibit otherwise it would be deemed 'not according to the schedule'. The expression is being superseded by the word integrate in the compiling of show schedules.
See also *Feature* and *Integrate*

Incurved
Petals or florets of a flower curving inwards, especially Chrysanthemums.

Indefinite inflorescence
Alternative expression for racemose inflorescence.

Indehiscent
Not opening to allow seeds to escape, eg nuts.

Independent assortment, Law of
Mendel's second law which states that most of the characteristics of the parents can appear in any combination in their offspring.

Indigenous plant
A species that occurs naturally in a country as distinct from one introduced by man.

Indirect line
A 'broken' line, interrupted with shapes or forms or points, which can be connected or not.
See also *Lines of continuance*

Indumentation
The arrangement of hairs or down on a plant.

Induplicate
Parts of a bud bent or folded inwards with the edges touching but not overlapping.

Inferior
A structure that is positioned below another structure – an ovary is described as inferior when located below the point of attachment of the perianth and stamens.
See also *Superior*

Inflorescence
A particular arrangement of flowers on the main stalk of a plant. Classified into two groups:
(1) racemose, (2) cymose.
Racemose is where the oldest flower is at the base and there are progressively younger flowers towards the tip.
Cymose the oldest flower is terminal and the younger flowers appear lower down the stalk. See also *Cyme*

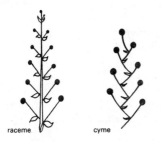

raceme   cyme

Informal
Not an official occasion and where floral arrangements would reflect the ambience of a casual gathering.

Informal tribute
A funeral tribute; includes the spray, sympathy (cremation) basket, coffin and casket spray or a sheaf of flowers.

Inhibition
The prevention or slowing down of a reaction (1) by temperatures that are too high or too low or (2) by the treatment of certain chemicals, eg retarding the opening of flowers by cold room storage.

Initial
One of a group of cells that divides to produce the cells of plant tissue. The cells of cambium, cork cambium and the apical meristem are initials.

Inorganic
(1) Compounds which do not contain carbon, (2) Not having the structure or characteristics of living organisms, eg inorganic fertilizers.
See also *Organic*

Insecticide
Any substance, natural or chemical which is toxic to insects.

Inspiration
Stimulation of the mind or feelings towards creativity and the beginning of a composition or design. Nature is the greatest source of inspiration but other ideas can stimulate flower arrangers such as works of painters, historical periods, poems, etc.

Integrate
To incorporate or unify with a larger unit or design; applied use of accessories should be seen to be within, or part of the design and not placed in isolation or as an afterthought.
See also *Feature* and *Incorporate*

Integument
The outer protective covering of an ovule which becomes the coat of the

seed (testa) once it is fertilized. It is perforated by a small pore (micropyle). See also *Testa*

Internal wiring
Method of wiring whereby the support wiring is inserted up a hollow or soft fleshy stem thus concealing the wire and obviating the need for prior taping. See also *Double internal wiring*

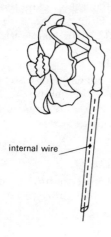

internal wire

Internode
Portion of stem between two nodes. See also *Node*

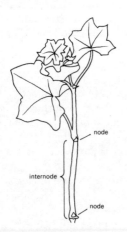

node

internode

node

Interphase
The period following the completion of one cell division and the next.

Interpretation
The representation of a theme called for by a class title; use of predominating and appropriate plant material along with other components in order to convey the atmosphere and illustrate the concept.

Interpretive
A design which uses principles and elements in such a way as to require an emotional and visual response to a theme.

Introrse
Facing inwards, eg anthers which open and shed their pollen towards the axis of the flower (opposite of extrorse).

Involucre
One or more whorls of bracts immediately below a flower, fruit or inflorescence with a capitulum or an umbel.

Iridaceae   P3+3 or (3+3) A3 $\bar{G}(3)$
Large family (5 tribes) of monocotyledons includes Sisyrinchium, Iris, Ixia, Crocus, Gladiolus.

Iridescent
Producing a display of lustrous rainbow-like colours such as mother-of-pearl (the inside layer of certain mollusc shells).

Irregular
(1) Flowers having any of their parts, especially petals, differing in size, shape, etc, ie asymmetrical (same as zygomorphic) or

(2) a set of organs of similar function but which differ in structure among themselves.

Isosceles triangle
Outline or basic shape of an arrangement or design where the base is shorter than the two equal sides of the triangle forming the apex.

J

Jack-in-the-Green
An arrangement of the flowers of the Primrose and Polyanthus where the bloom has a Tudor 'ruff' or row of green petals beneath.
See also *Hose-in-hose*

Judging
The careful assessment or evaluation of exhibits in a show in order to place the prize winners and award trophies.

The skill demands a wide knowledge, ethics, integrity and experience in the field of flower arranging and/or floristry. NAFAS organizes Area and National Judging qualifications as does the Society of Floristry and other organizations like the W.I.

Juglandaceae   P4 A3-40 G̅2
A small family of trees, which includes Hickory and Walnut.

K

K
The symbol for calyx in floral formula.

Keel
Partly joined petals forming a 'boat shaped' arrangement within which are the stamens. Characteristic of the family Papilionaceae which includes Lupin and Sweet Pea.

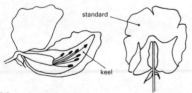

Kernel
The seed in a drupe.

Key
The winged seed pod of Ash, Lime and Sycamore – another name for *samara*.

Kind
'Three different kinds' (of flowers or plants) a popular expression in show schedules for genus and means that plants or flowers should vary from one another botanically.

Kinetic design
A design related to the branch of

dynamics which deals with matter in motion as opposed to static matter. Kinetic designs include Stabiles, Mobiles and Stamobiles as well as the more modern concepts of Op Art and psychedelic designs.

Kitchen garden
Although simply a garden where vegetables and some soft fruits are grown, the kitchen garden has its origins in antiquity (the 4th millennium BC) in the Near East. Probably introduced into Britain by the Romans.

The kitchen garden became walled in Tudor times and flourished from the 17th to the 19th centuries. Beds were laid out beneath the walls, and paths separated the 'quarters' which were cultivated in rotation.

Knot garden
Part of a garden planted in the form of a geometrical design of intricate patterns. Popular in the 16th and 17th centuries.

Originally the low-growing herbs of Thyme and Hyssop were used for edging knot gardens but they were superseded in the late 16th century by the dwarf Box (Buxus Sempervirens 'Suffruticosa'). Coloured sands and gravel or shell paths separated the 'ribbons'.

L

Labiatae K(5) C(5) A2-4 G2
A large family of 8 tribes includes
Monarda, Perovskia, Molucella,
Lamium, Stachys, Phlomis, Teucrium,
Marrubium, Ajuga, Lavandula and
many aromatic and culinary herbs
such as mint, sage, thyme etc.

Labyrinth
See *Maze*

Lacerate
Leaf form which is torn, irregularly
cut or jagged.

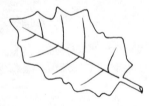

Laciniate
Leaf margin dissected into narrow
pointed segments.

Lamina
The thin flattened blade of a leaf
either side of the midrib.
See also *Blade*

Lanceolate
Leaf shape with curved edges
narrowing to the base and apex in the
manner of a lance-head; the length at
least three times longer than the
breadth.

Landscape
A design which represents a natural
scene; depicts nature as far as
practical and is related to it in scale
and use of plant material. The scale of
accessories is an important aspect as
is that of the overall exhibit.

Landscape architecture
The art of laying out grounds and
designing and integrating natural
and man-made features in harmony.

Landscape architecture ranges from large scale major projects of new towns, motorways, reservoirs, etc, to the smallest garden design.

Lanuginose

Woolly or covered in fine hairs.

Lateral

A side shoot, branch, or root, as distinct from the leader.
See also *Leader*

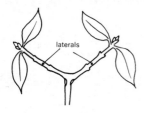

Latex

A whitish milky fluid containing protein, starch, etc, found in some herbaceous plants and trees. In conditioning such plant material the ends of the cut stem must be singed with a flame, eg Euphorbia var.

Laurel (Prunus laurocerasus)

A very important foliage for the florist for use as green foundation work especially for Armed Services funerals and Chaplet designs. It is also used as a backing for mossed bases and it can be pinned, pleated or curled.

Law of Colour Areas

A small amount of strong colour balances a larger area of weak colour. Small areas of pure colour are more acceptable than large ones because pure colour is more exciting, even if tiring, to the eye.

Law of Unity

The major agreement or minor contrast in a design. In simpler terms: one dominant feature with a contrasting one of a similar nature.

Lawn

A characteristic of an English garden and generally a flat area of cultivated grass which has to be mown regularly. Lawns can be mown into patterns by varying the height of the cutting blades.

In medieval times, lawns made of Camomile (Anthemis nobilis) were popular. They are coming back into fashion since such lawns are both fragrant and mat-forming.

Lax

Having loosely arranged parts such as a flower cluster.

Layering

The method of vegetatively propagating certain subjects by (1) stem, (2) air, (3) tip layering. Shoots are kept attached to mother plant until rooted when they are severed, lifted and re-planted.

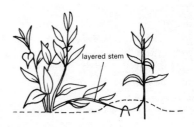

Leader

A shoot which has grown naturally and has been selected to extend the branch framework of a tree or shrub to improve or purposely train its shape.

Leadwork

Cisterns, statuary, vases and urns cast in lead from moulds. A decorative feature of garden ornament dating from the 17th and 18th centuries. An alternative to stone statuary providing a focal point in a minor setting.

Leaf

The plant organ whose function is photosynthesis and transpiration. Each leaf has a lateral bud in its axil. Leaves are arranged in a definite pattern, and show considerable variation in size, shape, arrangement of veins, texture and attachment to stem. Leaves may also be modified for special purposes.

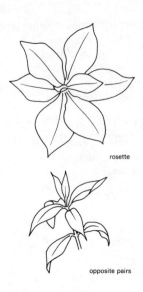

rosette

opposite pairs

Leaflet

One of the small leaf-like divisions of a compound leaf.

Leaf mosaic

The arrangement of leaves on a stem as viewed in plan form demonstrating a plant's ability to secure the maximum exposure of the leaf to light and air. NOT to be confused with mosaic disease.

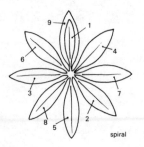

spiral

Leaf shine

Proprietary liquids which are sprayed or wiped on to remove dust from leaves and impart a glossy look to the leaves. For houseplants, cut foliage or such like.

Leaf structure (internal)

A dicotyledon leaf comprises upper (adaxial) and lower (abaxial) epidermis which are single layers of tabular cells giving mechanical protection to the mesophyll and preventing excess evaporation. In turn these epidermis cells are protected by cuticles formed from a waxy substance – cutin. The tissue between the epidermis is the mesophyll in which the veins are embedded. Mespophyll is differentiated into palisade tissue and spongy mesophyll. The principal activity of photosynthesis occurs in palisade cells. Within the spongy mesophyll are large air spaces. The stomata are mostly on the underside (abaxial) surface of the leaf.

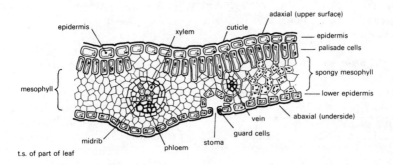

t.s. of part of leaf

Legume
A dehiscent pod formed from a single carpel, containing seeds which are shed when mature. It splits along both sides and is the fruit of the family Leguminosae. (Lupin, Laburnum, Pea family).

Leguminosae   K4-5 or (4-5)
  C5 A4-∞ G̲1
A very large family of great economic importance (peas, beans, etc) having the ability to make their own nitrogen from nodules on the root. Flowers include the Sweet Pea and Lupin and the shrubs – Cytisus (Broom), Genista, Laburnum, Robinia, Wistaria, Gleditschia.

Lenticel
A raised pore on the stems of woody plants allowing gas exchange between the atmosphere and the internal tissue.

Leucoplast
A plastid containing no pigment (ie colourless) and used by plants to store starch grains. If leucoplasts are exposed to light they form toxins, as when potatoes go green.

Lichens
A group consisting of organisms that are symbiotic between a green or blue-green alga and a fungus. They are slow growing and can live in areas that are too cold or exposed for other plants. The alga photosynthesizes and passes its food to the fungus which in turn protects the algal cells.

In competitive work lichens are acceptable as either fresh or dried plant material and need not be staged in water. See aslo *Symbiosis*

Lichen moss   (also known as
  Icelandic or Reindeer moss)
A decorative but expensive imported moss which has to be soaked before use and can be used as foundation on a frame, to embellish a design, or to mask mechanics in an arrangement.

Life cycle
The complete sequence of changes through which a stage in the life of an organism progresses to the same stage in the life of its offspring.

Lifting
The digging up of plants for replanting elsewhere. Lifting should be done

at the time of the year appropriate for the type of plant or shrub and should generally take place during the Spring or Autumn months.

Light blue

A tint of blue, the colour of Wedgwood pottery and a colour for Rococo period work.

Opt app	Psycho eff	Symb interp
light	soothing	romance
floating	refreshing	serenity
hazy	contemplative	peace
airy		
soft		

Lights

Rebated frames of wood which house glass in order to cover a low brick or timber construction having sloping sides.
Dutch light – single piece of glass 1420 mm x 730 mm
English light – 1829 mm x 1219 mm with glazing bars in which small panes of glass are fixed. See also *Frame*

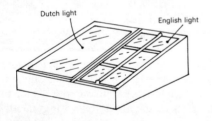

Dutch light

English light

Lignin

A complex compound which is deposited in the cellulose cell walls of the xylem and sclerenchyma during secondary thickening. Lignification makes the walls woody and is especially noticeable in old plants. It also helps to preserve wood from infection, rot and decay.

Ligule

(1) A strap-like extension (ray floret) of the corolla in a composite inflorescence (capitulum).
(2) A thin flap of tissue at the base of a leaf blade in many grasses.

Liliaceae   P3+3 A6 G3

A very large family of monocotyledons with 16 tribes; includes Alliums Fritillaria, Colchicum, Agapanthus, Hosta, Polygonatum, Asphodelus, Tulip, Eucomis, Galtonia, Hyacinth, etc.

Lime-hating   (calcifuges)

Plants which grow in soil conditions requiring an acid soil of pH below 7. Most heathers, Magnolia, Rhododendrons and Pieris are lime-hating plants.

Lime-tolerant   (calciphiles)

Plants which grow in soil conditions with an alkali pH above 7 such as Prunus, Scabious, Syringa, Acanthus and some Heathers (Erica carnea).

Line

A very expressive aspect in design, being a form which attracts the eye to move along it. Lines can be very rhythmic in quality and can express many moods as well as represent physical qualities.

Line arrangement

A design in which 'line' plant material is dominant, where in terms

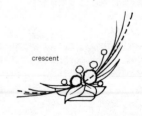

crescent

of proportion the voids exceed the solids, and where the visual movement is in the form of a line which can be vertical, horizontal, crescent, curved, spiral, diagonal or Hogarth shape.
See also *Outline*

vertical

Linear
Leaf shape that is long and very narrow with nearly parallel margins and narrowing at the base like a blade of grass.

Lines of Continuance
Imaginary lines or visual paths which take the eye through a design of floral art but of which nothing tangible delineates the path.

lines of continuance

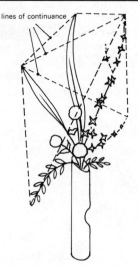

Linnaean system
See *Binomial nomenclature*

Lips
The two main divisions of an irregular corolla where the upper part forms a hood or shield for the stamens and the lower platform on which insects alight.

Liverwort
A plant of the Bryophtya division which grows in wet conditions and resembles green sea-weed. In the class of hepaticopsida (formerly hepaticae).

Lobed
Leaf margins divided into segments, the spaces between which do not reach the axis or centre.

95

Local colour

The actual colour of an object or area. The effect of shadow, light and reflection from nearby objects reduces its pure hue substantially but shadows contain some of the complementary colour of the object.

Locule   (loculus)

The cavity of the ovary containing the ovules. The loculi of the anther contain the developing pollen grains.

locule

Long-day plant

A plant whose flowering can be induced or prolonged by long days, usually by giving more than 12 hours of daylight by means of artificial lighting.

Longitudinal section

A cut made through or along an organ or tissue in the same direction as its growth in order to study structure. Abbreviated to L.S.
See also *Transverse section*

Loofah

The fibrous interior of the fruit of the dishcloth gourd (Luffa cylindrica) which is dried and bleached. It is dried plant material in floral art terms and is often confused with a marine animal such as sponge.

Loop (or crook) stage

An early stage or growth in allium type seedlings where the growing tip

is still bent over and held by the seed coat.

Loop-method   (wiring)

Wiring method used for securing small pieces of Cupressus foliage (or similar) together for edging formal designs of funeral tributes.

Loose posy   (or open posy)

A bouquet in a round design which is very appropriate for a child bridesmaid. It is made up from a selection of mixed flowers and foliage in scale. The size of finished posy depends on the age of the child.

Loose work   (opposite of massed foundation work)

The use of flowers in funeral designs, either in one or several kinds and colours, assembled openly so that they stand away from the frame. The taller flowers are selected for the central line or circle. Other flowers are not positioned close to each other but can be arranged freely or in pattern, but the outline shape of the tribute must be retained. The spaces between the flowers are filled with foliage and the frame greened.

Low-key

A design or arrangement having a predominance of dark grey tones or

dark colours without highlights.
See also *High-key*

Luminosity (of colour)
The extent to which a colour appears
to emit or reflect light. It is the quality
which makes some colours more
visible than others in poor light.

In average daylight the order of
luminosity is: Yellow, Yellow/
orange, Yellow/green, Orange/
green, Red/orange, Blue, Blue/green,
Red/violet, Red, Blue/violet and
Violet.

Lustrous
Shining or glossy; a surface texture

appearance which is more dominant
than a dull one.

Lyrate
A pinnatifid leaf in which the
terminal lobe is the largest.

M

Made-up plant material
Assembly of component parts of dried plant material (including wood) into simulated flowers, fruit, etc, which may be glued, wired and/or taped and coloured. Non-natural materials such as artificial stamens, berries, etc, may NOT be used in the assembly of flowers, etc, when used in competitive work, *unless* artificial plant material is permitted in the show schedule.

Magenta
A deep purplish-red named after the battle of Magenta 1859. It is one of the three process colours in colour reproduction (with Yellow and Cyan).

Magnoliaceae K3 C6 – ∞ A∞ $\underline{G}$∞
A family of woody plants including Magnolia and Liriodendron (Tulip Tree).

Maiden tree
A tree in its first year after grafting or budding, and consisting of a single unbranched stem.

Male flower
A flower having stamens but with the ovary absent or rudimentary.

Malmaison
Large carnation buttonhole created from three carnations, (which have had their seed boxes removed), and then assembled on a thin card backing along with 7 or 8 wired small leaves and 6 carnation leaves.

The typical Malmaison carnation is massive and has a very large centre composed of small petals. Named Souvenir de la Malmaison after the Empress Josephine's garden at Château de Malmaison which was famous for its roses.

Malvaceae K5 or (5) C5 A(∞)
  $\underline{G}$(1-∞)
A small family of woody shrubs such as Hibiscus and Lavatera arborea (Tree Mallow) as well as Herbaceous Althaea (Hollyhock), Sidalcea, Lavatera and Malva.

Marble
A hard crystalline metamorphic rock which can be fashioned into bases or figurines and highly polished.

Margin
The edge of a leaf or flower.

Mass
A classification of floral art designs where the plant material is used in quantity with little use of space in the design. It is the style of some Historical Periods, traditional and geometric mass designs.

Matt
A dull surface without sheen that

does not reflect light efficiently. It is a textural quality of a surface.

Maze
A complex network of paths generally bordered with tall hedges designed to create a puzzle in order to get to the centre. The best known example is at Hampton Court which is dated *c* 1690.

Mechanics
The use of pinholders, frogs, wire, wire netting, tape, clay and twine as a physical means of securing the plant material so that it remains stable and balanced. An important basic skill requirement of all floristry and flower arranging. Mechanics should always be hidden and technically sound to obviate either plant material falling over or the whole arrangement collapsing.

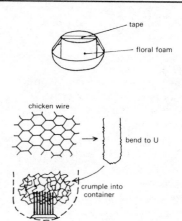

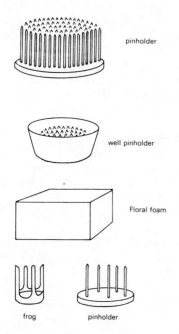

Medium
The solid or liquid substrate containing all the materials (eg compost, Perlite, etc) necessary for plant growth and for the growth of tissue cultures in micro-propagation.

Medullary ray   (or vascular ray)
Any of the vertical plates of parenchyma cells running radially through the cylinder of vascular tissue. Medullary rays store and transport food material.

Megaphyllous
Having large leaves (also macrophyllous).

Meiosis   (or reduction division)
A type of cell division that results in four reproductive cells, each with half the chromosome number of the parent cell. Meiosis occurs in all organisms which reproduce sexually.

Membrane
Thin sheet of soft fibrous tissue that covers and protects cells and organelles and also controls movement of substances in and out of them. Membranes are permeable to water

and fat soluble substances but impermeable to sugars.

Mendel's Laws
The two laws of inheritance produced by Mendel, the Law of Segregation and the Law of Independent Assortment.
See also *Segregation, Law of* and *Independent Assortment, Law of*

Meristem
Any tissue of actively dividing cells which produces the cells of other plant tissues. Meristems in the apex of stems or roots are called apical. The meristem between the xylem and phloem is called the cambium.

Meristem culture is the micropropagation under clinical conditions which produces virus-free plants and those which are otherwise difficult to propagate.
See also *Xylem, Phloem* and *Cambium*

Meristematic
Young cells in growing points of stems or roots which divide into two and each of these may divide again. The process repeats and cells gradually add to the body of the organism. Mature cells do not normally divide, unless to form cambium or produce protective tissues after injury.

Mesocarp
The central part of the pericarp which is often fleshy, especially in drupes.

Mesophyll
The internal tissue of a leaf blade consisting of parenchyma cells in two distinct forms, pallisade and mesophyll, just beneath the upper

epidermis and spongy mesophyll. It occupies the remainder of the lamina.
See also *Leaf*

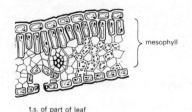

t.s. of part of leaf

Mesophyte
Any plant adapted to moderate conditions of soil which is well supplied with water and mineral salts. Most flowering plants are mesophytes.
See also *Xerophyte* and *Hydrophyte*

Micro climate
The climate of a small or limited space in a terrarium, bottle garden or propagating frame; or the climate created for a small collection of house plants having moist conditions around the surfaces of leaves.

Micro-organism
Any small, microscopic organism such as bacteria, virus.

Micropyle
A very small opening in the seed coat (testa) of most seeds through which water is absorbed at the beginning of germination. The weak spot where the radicle emerges. Also the hollow tube or pore at the tip of the ovule through which the pollen enters.

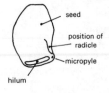

Midrib
The largest vein of a leaf usually running lengthwise along the axis from base to apex.

Mildew
A disease of plants caused by a fungus growing on the surface of soil, leaves or petals. There are two types of mildew viz downy and powdery.

Miniature
A class for an exhibit which must not exceed 102 mm in height, depth and width. It should theoretically be possible to place the exhibit within a cube of those dimensions. NB The diagonal measurements can exceed 102 mm.

Minimal art
An extreme form of Abstract art relying upon simple form and flat colour for effect. Not intended to represent an object or emotion.

Mist propagation
Propagation of stem cuttings by spraying them with a fine mist periodically so that a film of water is maintained on the leaves. Mist is controlled either by time pulse or by photo-electric cells. A soil-warming facility is also required in order to give warmth to promote root growth.

Mitosis
The normal process of cell-division, by vegetative or somatic means, which replicates a cell exactly such that the offspring have the same number of chromosomes as the parent.

Mobile
An assembly of plant material which is designed to be suspended. All the component parts must move freely with air movement, thus creating changing patterns. It is an art form of moving sculpture where each element is suspended by its own wire or string and these in turn are attached to central supports. An American, Alexander Calder (1898-1976) invented this kind of kinetic sculpture in the 1930s and used nature as his inspiration for metal mobiles.
See also *Stabile* and *Stamobile*

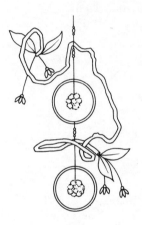

Modern
A contemporary design, influenced by the free form style. Bold, with dramatic impact, the designs are made using plant materials economically, sometimes in unusual combinations. Space is integrated with an open silhouette outline. All components should be in the appropriate style. Little or no transition material. Balance is always dynamic and may be symmetrical or asymmetrical. Some distortion of plant material, curled and cut leaves, etc, is allowed but it is always used as it grows, ie

101

there is no complete abstraction of material.

Monadelphous
Having all the stamens joined together in a tube or bundle which surrounds the style.

Monocarpic
Plants which produce fruit only once in their life-cycle such as most annual plants. See also *Polycarpic*

Monochasium
A cymose inflorescence where one branch grows out from below the first flower and in turn this terminates in a flower.

 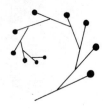

Monochromatic
Gradations of one colour or hue only, using tints, shades or tones. Monochromatic colours are related harmonies.

Monocotyledonae
One of the two classes of plants within the sub-division Angiospermae having one seed leaf (cotyledon) within the seed. Generally, monocotyledons have parallel leaf veins, flower parts in threes or multiples thereof and scattered vascular bundles within the stems. Bulbs, lilies, tulips, onions, grasses are all examples.
See also *Dicotyledon*

Monoecious
Plant species that have separate male and female flowers on the same plant, eg Hazel (Corylus avellana).
See also *Dioecious*

Monopodial
Type of branching where the main axis of the plant is the original shoot apex with lateral branches growing out from it. The growth of the main axis causes the increase in height of the plant.
See also *Dichotomous* and *Sympodial*

Monotypic
Consisting of only one type of plant single species, genus.

Montage
Collage made up of printed or photographed images making a composite total image.

Moraine
A form of alpine (rock) gardening where a bed of rock debris emulates the ridges and mounds of glacial action. It requires a very stony structure with a well-drained rooting medium of some depth.

Morphology
The branch of botany concerned with the form and structure of organisms.

Mosaic disease
Certain viral infections which cause irregular patterns on leaves reducing the plant's ability to make chlorophyll.

Moss (musci)
A class of plants within the division Bryophyta found in both damp and drier conditions.

See also *Bun moss, Reindeer moss* and *Sphagnum moss*

Mossing
The binding of moss to a funeral frame with either string or wire in order to make up a base to hold the wired flowers and foliage. The moss should be teased and all debris removed before using.

Mothering Sunday
The fourth Sunday in Lent when traditionally children give gifts to their mothers. Flowers, flowering plants and posies feature significantly in their choice of gift.

Mother's Day
An American custom held annually on 8 May but the term is now commonly used in the UK for Mothering Sunday.

Motif
A repeated figure or design in architecture or decoration, eg the acanthus leaf in Classical Greek architecture.

Mould
A rough, variously coloured coating caused by the action of saprophytic fungi. The general name for a fungal growth on the surface of soil or on fruit and flowers.

Mount
A garden feature of medieval origin, surviving into the 18th century, which provided a good vantage point.

Mounting
(1) The means of securing dried wood or driftwood to a base by use of 'Polyfilla' mixture or other techniques of wiring and screwing supports.
(2) A form of wiring (adding wire legs) so that the stems of flowers and leaves can be inserted into mossed foundations or wired into any shape required. The leg made by the mounting wire may be single or double: the double-leg ensures a firmer anchorage into based work.

Mucronate
Leaf apex ending abruptly in a short stiff point.

Muff spray
In winter, bridesmaids may carry a muff in which case a spray of flowers attached to it is an alternative to a bouquet.

Mulch
A top dressing put on top of the soil around plants to conserve moisture. The soil should be damp before adding the mulch which can be decomposing leaf-mould, peat, well-rotted manure, or lawn mowings. May is the best month for mulching. Black polythene plastic sheeting, used to conserve moisture, and suppress weeds is another form of mulching.

Multicellular
Made up of many cells as in most plants.

Mushroom

Any of various fleshly fruiting bodies produced by the class Basidiomycetes fungi (of the family Agaricaceae). See also *Toadstool*

Mutation

Sudden and permanent change in the reproductive cells of a plant, which can be useful, harmless or cause the death of a plant. Mutations result in variation between individual plants.

Mycelium

The vegetative part of a fungus consisting of a mass of threadlike filaments called *hyphae*.

Mycorrhiza

The symbiotic association of the mycelium of a fungus with the roots of certain plants. Plants with mycorrhizae often grow faster because they are provided with extra nutrients by the mycorrhizae.

Myrtaceae K4-5 or (4-5) C4-5 A∞ G1-∞

A family of aromatic evergreen trees or shrubs, including Eucalyptus and Myrtus (Myrtle).

N

NAFAS
The National Association of Flower Arrangement Societies of Great Britain. An association of Flower Clubs of Great Britain with headquarters at 21 Denbigh Street, London SW1V 2HF. The country is divided into 20 Area Associations each with its own officers. There is an Overseas Area affiliated to NAFAS.

NAFAS publish *The Flower Arranger*, a quarterly magazine and annually organize a National Festival and a display stand at the Chelsea Flower Show as well as other activities.

NAFAS frames the rules for all competitive work and tests Judges, Speakers and Demonstrators to Area and National standards. It was formed in 1959. At present (1988) there are about 1400 Clubs with a membership of 100,000.

Naked
Without hairs or scales; seeds not enclosed in a pericarp; flowers lacking a perianth.

Nappe
The smooth sheet of water that flows over a dam or weir into an ornamental basin.

National Council for the Conservation of Plants and Gardens (NCCPG)
Formed in 1979 to protect species which are in danger of going out of cultivation. Collections are being established in various Botanic Gardens, Nurseries and gardens of the National Trust, etc. Local branches at County level have been formed.

National Trust (NT)
An organization concerned with the preservation of Historic Buildings and Gardens as well as large tracts of countryside. Founded in 1895 and incorporated in an act of Parliament in 1907. The NT for Scotland was founded in 1931.

Natural flowers
Flowers in their natural state, namely grown and picked without being preserved, painted, pipped or feathered.

Natural funeral bunch (sheaf)
A tribute where the flowers are not wired and the bunch is made up in the hand to be a facing arrangement. It is possible for the flowers to be placed directly into a vase in church after the service.

Natural group
A group of plants which share many characteristics and are thought to have a common ancestor.

Naturalise
The growing of plants under con-

ditions allowing them to grow and increase without maintenance, eg snowdrops and daffodils in woodland areas.

Natural order
The former name for a family in the classification of plants.

Natural plant material
Flowers, foliage, berries, fruit, etc, which are either fresh (living) or preserved by any method.

Natural unit
An assembly of flowers and/or foliage on their own stems and where two or more are mounted together and subsequently used in a design.

Nautilus
A mollusc, found in the Indian and Pacific Oceans, which has a shell with a series of air filled chambers.

Near Complementary Colour
A colour relationship which exists

between a colour and ONE of the two colours which lies either side of its complementary colour. It is a contrasting harmony of two hues, eg
(a) Blue and Yellow/orange or Red/orange;
(b) Violet and Yellow/green or Yellow/orange.

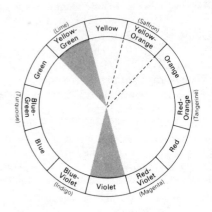

Nectar
A sugary liquid attracting pollinating insects – which is produced in the flowers of plants by their nectaries.

Needle
A long thin leaf of some conifers.

Needle-point holders
An alternative, but out-dated, term for pinholders used in mechanics for flower arranging. The word originated in America.

Negative space
An essential aspect of Abstract work being the space around and between the materials used. It is as important

as positive space in such designs.
See also *Positive space*

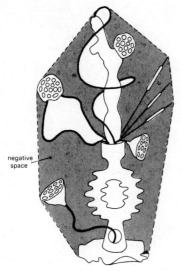

negative
space

Nerve
The large, most prominent vein in a leaf.

Net venation
The arrangement of veins in a leaf from one main vein (or in some cases several main veins) to thinner branch veins to even smaller, thinner veins, etc, giving the appearance of a fine network. Such leaves can in some

cases be 'skeletonized' for floral art purposes, eg Magnolia leaves.

Neutral colour
See *Achromatic colour*

Niche
(1) A recessed space created by a backboard with sides into which staged exhibits are placed in competitive work. Sometimes referred to as an alcove. Sizes of niches are generally stated in show schedules as are other conditions of staging.
(2) Also a recess in a wall especially to house a statue or protect an important feature.

Nicotine
A poisonous, colourless, alkaloid present in tobacco and used as an insecticide.

Nitrate (NO$_3$)
An inorganic substance in the soil which is an important nutrient for plants.

Nitrogen
Symbol N, an essential constituent of proteins and nucleic acid in living organisms. Nitrogen occurs in the air (*c* 78% by volume) and also naturally in organic matter as plant and animal remains.

Nitrogen cycle
One of the major cycles of chemical elements in the ecosystem. Nitrates in the soil are taken up by plant roots, converted to protein and eaten by animals which excrete waste products back into the soil as manure.

Decomposing bacteria in the soil break down the organic compounds into nitrate and ammonia, the former

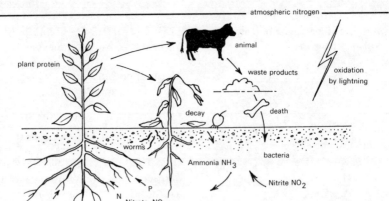

being taken up by oxidation. Some combined nitrogen is also set free by denitrifying bacteria.

Node
The point on a stem from which a leaf grows. The space between nodes on a stem is called an *internode*.

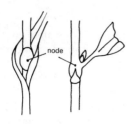

Nodule
A swelling caused by bacteria which is involved in nitrogen fixation on the roots of a member of the Leguminosae family of plants, eg Sweet Peas.

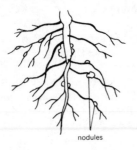

nodules

Not according to schedule
The appropriate way in which NAFAS judges write a comment if the exhibit is eliminated for consideration for a prize because it does not conform to the schedule, viz:
(1) The exhibit exceeds the space allowed or does not comply with any specific requirements, eg components required or expressly forbidden;
(2) if any fresh plant material is not in water or water-retaining material;
(3) if the exhibit includes artificial plant material when it is not permitted.

Notched
Petals which are shallowly indented at their outer end.

Nucellus
The tissue that makes up the greater part of the ovule of speed plants. It contains the embryo sac and is enclosed by the integuments except for the micropyle.

Nuclear membrane
The membrane around the nucleus of a cell, having two layers and many pores connecting the nucleoplasm with the cytoplasm.
See also *Cytoplasm* and *Nucleoplasm*

Nucleic acid
There are two kinds of nucleic acid which are found in the cells of all living organisms namely DNA and RNA. See also *DNA* and *RNA*

Nucleoplasm
The protoplasm inside the nucleus of a cell which contains the chromosomes and the nucleoli.

Nucleus
Controls most of the activities of the cell. The nucleus contains DNA, the only known chemical that can double itself without anything making it.

Nut
A dry (indehiscent) fruit with a hard wall that does not split open and contains one seed.

Nutation
The spiral movement of a plant organ during growth as in climbing plants. Helps the plant to find suitable supports to twine around. The tendrils of Sweet Peas exemplify.

Nutrient
Mineral substances absorbed by the roots, or leaves of plants and needed for healthy growth.

Nutrition
The process of taking up nutrients and using them in chemical reactions (metabolism) to manufacture foods; known as *holophytic nutrition*.

O

Oasis-fix
A brand-name, oil-based adhesive which can be manipulated to fix mechanics, and secure candle-cups in candlesticks, etc. It does not harden and dry out.

Obelisk
A garden ornament or feature of historical origin. It declined in popularity in private English gardens in the 19th century. It has a square or rectangular cross section with sides that taper towards a pyramidal top.

Objet d'art
A small object considered to be of artistic merit with its function subordinate to the decorative value.

Objet trouvé
An object coming to notice by chance; not looked for; can be of natural forms such as driftwood but must be aesthetically significant.

Oblanceolate
A leaf shape which is inversely lanceolate.

Obligate
Able to exist under only one set of environmental conditions; essential.

Oblique
Leaf base which has asymmetrical sides.

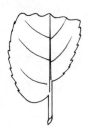

Oblong
A simple leaf shape, with almost parallel sides where the length is longer than the width.

Obovate
A leaf shape which is ovate with the broadest part beyond the middle of the blade.

Obtuse
A leaf apex ending in a blunt tip.

Offset
Complete but smaller plants produced alongside and attached to the parent plant which are capable of taking root when separated. Bulbs and corms form offsets.

Oleaceae   K(4) C(4-6) or o A2 G̲(2)
A very large family of trees and shrubs which includes Ash (Fraxinus) Forsythia, Jasminum, Ligustrum, Osmanthus and Syringa.

Onagraceae   K4 C4 A2-8 Ḡ(4)
Small family of herbaceous perennials including Epilobium and Oenothera.

Op art
Optical art, an important movement of the 1960s. Not concerned with pictorial representation but instead utilizing pattern, colour and shape to create a disturbing impact on the retina, giving sensations of move- ment. Majority of paintings are in black and white.

Open book
Funeral tribute in the shape of an open book, though the design is a massed one, not 'open'. The frame is constructed like a cushion with a flat base and curved top already welded on and, therefore, difficult to moss. The top of the design is based in white flowers and the edges of the frame are covered with small gold coloured flowers or foliage to represent the gilding of a book.

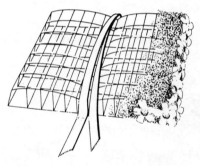

Open weather
Periods in winter that are free from frost, snow or rain.

Opposite
An arrangement of two leaves which arise at the same node but on either side of a stem. See also *Alternate*

Optical effect (of colour)

The visual impression that certain colours give, such as certain characteristics of 'temperature', recession, clarity, weight, etc.

Optical mixing

The sensation caused when eye and brain involuntarily mix small juxtaposed areas of pure colour into bigger areas of secondary colour.

Orange

A secondary colour obtained from the mixture of yellow and red pigments.
Zodiac: Leo

   Heraldry: Tenne. Strength and
      Endurance
   effect under tungsten light: slightly
      deeper
   effect under white fluorescent light:
      yellowish-orange

Opt app	Psycho eff	Symb interp
warmth	excitement	sun
vitality	activity	courage
advancing	joyful	cordiality
shining	warming	communicative
soft	strength	ripeness/
dry	energetic	maturity
penetrating		autumn
restful	hopeful	

Orangery

Earliest examples in England date from the end of the 16th century, and are elaborate buildings, sometimes part of the main dwelling house, (Bowood, Wilts) or quite separate (Heveningham Hall, Suffolk, 1779). Built in classical styles or in the 'decorative' fashion of the period as glass-walled enclosures in which to grow oranges. They also gave shelter to other tender plants which had been collected by the plant hunters.

Orbicular

A simple leaf shape which is circular in outline.

Order

A 'fifth order' category (including subdivision and subclass) in the classification of plants in the Plant Kingdom consisting of families. The Latin names of orders usually end in -ales.

Order	Plants
Taxales	Yews
Coniferales	Pines, Cypressus, Redwoods
Rosales	Roses, Saxifrages, Peas
Ranales	Buttercups, Berberis

Organ

A group of cells or tissues forming part of an organism with a specialized function, eg root, leaf.

Organic

(1) Compounds which contain atoms of carbon.
(2) Characteristic of living plants.
(3) Fertilizers or pesticides derived from animal or vegetable matter.

Organism

Any living plant which grows and reproduces.

Originality
The quality of being different, not copies but acceptable 'in the style of'. Exhibits in bad taste even if original should be discouraged.

Osmosis
The process whereby water moves through a semi-permeable membrane from a weaker to a concentrated solution. Occurs until both solutions are of the same concentration or until the osmotic pressure prevents it.

Outline
The visual aspect of a design suggesting the definition of the shape and sometimes expressed in geometric terms, viz triangle, circular, etc. It is the contour of an object.

Oval
Having the shape of an ellipse – broadest at the middle.

Ovary
The hollow base of the carpel of a flower containing one or more ovules. After fertilization the ovary wall develops into a fruit enclosing the seeds. Ovaries can be superior or inferior.

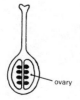

ovary

Ovate
A simple leaf shape which is egg-shaped in outline.

Ovate-acuminate egg-shaped to beyond the middle and then drawn out to a long narrow point

Ovate-deltoid – D shaped at base then ovate

Ovate-orbicular – nearly round but broadest below the middle.

Overall
From one end to another; refers to measurements in Miniature and Petite classes in show work. It is the measurement of height, width and depth but NOT any diagonal measurement.
See also *Miniature* and *Petite*

Overwiring
The use of either too many wires or wires that are too thick for the size of stem, flower or leaf. The result is a heavy and stiff design.

Ovoid
Egg-shaped with the broader end at the base such as fruit.

Ovule
The part of the female reproductive organs of seed plants consisting of nucellus, embryo sac and integuments. After fertilization the ovule

113

becomes a seed. There are several types of ovule placentation.
See also *Nucellus, Embryo sac,* and *Integuments*

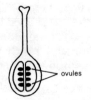

ovules

Ovum
An unfertilized egg-cell or female gamete.

Oxalidaceae K5 C5 A10 $\underline{G}$(5)
Family of one genus oxalis whose leaves fold up at night.

P

P

The symbol for perianth in the floral formulae eg Liliaceae P3+3 A6 $\underline{G}$(3). (Perianth segments petaloid)

Pagoda

A temple, usually in the form of a tower, pyramidal in shape and having many storeys. It originated in India and the Far East but copies were built in England as garden features or follies as the result of 'Oriental fever'. One famous surviving example is Chamber's pagoda in Kew Gardens erected in about 1760. Another is the pagoda fountain, *c* 1820, at Alton Towers, Staffs.

Painting

A method of colouring wood, leaves, fungi, etc, for use where dyed or painted natural plant material is permitted in a schedule.
See also *Spraying*

Paired Complementary Colour

A contrasting complement of four

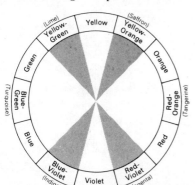

hues made up of two pairs of complementary colours in a close 'X' on the colour circle, eg Yellow/green and Yellow/orange plus Red/violet and Blue/violet.

Palisade parenchyma

A layer of upright cells below the upper epidermis in leaves, whose main function is photosynthesis.
See also *Leaf*

Palmate

A compound leaf shape with lobes or leaflets radiating from a point and spreading outwards.

Palmately lobed

Leaf shape where the midribs of the lobes are palmately arranged.

115

Palmately veined

Where the principal veins of a leaf are palmately arranged.

Palmette

A decoration resembling a fan-shaped palm leaf.

Palm house

A type of specially designed glass-house in which palms are grown. Botanic gardens feature such structures as attractions for the public – the palm house at Kew is a notable example.

Panicle

An inflorescence with stalked flowers branching from a central stem; a cluster of several branches each with numerous stalked flowers, eg Syringa (Lilac).

Paniculate

An inflorescence having flowers in panicles.

Papaveraceae K2-3 C4-6 A∞
$\underline{G}(2\text{-}\infty)$

Family of mostly annual or perennial herbaceous plants which includes Macleaya, Papaver (Poppy), Meconopsis. Romneya coulteri is the shrubby member.

Papier maché

Paper which is torn into small pieces and made into a pulp and then moulded over a former. When dry it forms a fairly lightweight durable object which can be painted and varnished.

Papilionaceae K(5)C5 or (5)
A10(10) or (9)+1 $\underline{G}$1

Family of eight tribes which includes Lupinus (Lupin), Trifolium (Clover), Galega (Goat's Rue), Lathyrus odoratus (Sweet Pea) and the shrubby members, as a sub-family of Leguminosae, are Cytisus (Broom), Genista, Laburnum and Spartium junceum (Yellow Spanish Broom).

Pappus

The hairs or bristles which replace the calyx in Compositae and Valerianaceae families.

Parallelism

The state of being parallel; an acceptable feature of Abstract work but considered a design fault in traditional designs. In certain circumstances it is used in contemporary 'nouvelle' designs.

Parallel venation

An arrangement of veins in a leaf where there is no main vein with

branches (net venation) but instead several veins, equal in size and running parallel to each other. The blade-like leaves of Iris, gladiolus, etc, and most monocotyledons have parallel veins.

Parasite
Plant (as well as insect) which lives on the resources of other living organisms (such as the mistletoe on apple trees).

Parchment
The skin of certain animals which is treated, dried and scraped to form a surface suitable for writing, as in medieval manuscripts. It is imitated in a type of stiff yellowish paper.
See also *Vellum*

Parenchyma
Plant tissues which are cells with thin walls, roughly spherical with air spaces between them. They appear in the cortex of stems and roots and the spongy mesophyll in leaves.

Paripinnate
A leaf which is pinnate but without an odd terminal leaflet.

Parted
Cut or cleft almost to the base.

Parterre
A formal garden of regular geometrical beds completely carpeted with low-growing plants or covered with (coloured) gravels. A style of French and Italian gardens of the 17th century, the designs were often edged with dwarf and clipped Box.

There are several other types and styles, eg *Parterres à l'anglaise* which were designs cut from turf, with gravel infilling.

Party flowers
Arrangements to suit the occasion and age group for which they are intended. The best choice is to have a few large-sized groups rather than several small arrangements which could be 'lost'. A sense of fun should prevail in the arrangements by using decorative ribbons, feathers, curled split-cane, etc.

Passage
A zone of transition in a work of art between certain tonal areas.

Pastel
A soft, delicate hue; a light tint.

Patina
Incrustation of the green oxidization on copper or bronze, formed as the surface ages; the sheen on the surface of antiques, caused by long handling or careful preservation.

Patio
The Spanish open inner courtyard, now a term used to describe a paved area adjoining a house for taking outdoor meals, etc.

Patte d'oie
'Goose-foot' – the point at which no

more than five straight avenues meet at acute angles in a parkland garden.

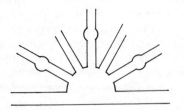

Pattern
An arrangement of repeated or corresponding parts. Nature creates so many patterns of its own such as a snowflake, a fir cone, the tide-washed sand, etc.

Peat
An organic mass of fibrous plant debris only partly decomposed and brown in colour. There are two types: *Moss peat* found near the surface of boggy areas and *Sedge peat*, older and darker brown with a higher water content. Peat is sterile and is useful for conditioning soil, to provide a mulch, or as a basis for mixing compost and grit as a rooting medium. Moss or sphagnum peats are usually very acid, more so than sedge peats.

Pectinate
Leaf margin shaped like a comb.

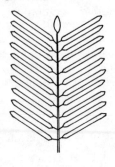

Pedestal
An elevated support for a base and container which may be in the manner of a column, one or more plinths or stands on which an arrangement is placed. Pedestal arrangements are a feature in churches, historic houses and competitive work. Generally the pedestal exhibit requires a lot of plant material. Most are large design, elegant and flamboyant in execution.

Pedicel
The stalk of a single flower in an inflorescence.

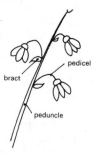

Peduncle
The main stalk of the whole inflorescence.

Pegboard
Hardboard perforated by a regular pattern of holes which is used for backboards, plaques and swags and covered with material if necessary. The holes are a means of attaching mechanics or accessories, etc.
See also *Hardboard*

Pegging
The use of dowelling to support and secure driftwood in a stable position.

Pellucid
Transparent or translucent.

Peltate
A leaf attached to the stalk by the centre or one face and not by the end, eg nasturtium.

Pendulous
Hanging downwards or 'weeping' as branches of certain trees.

Percée
Removal of a narrow avenue of trees in a wood so that an open view or vista is obtained.

Perennation
The ability of plants to live from one growing season to another by surviving the winter, which is a period of reduced activity. Bulbs, rhizomes, tubers and corms are examples.

Perennial
A plant (also including trees and shrubs) which lives and flowers for more than two years.

Perfoliate
A pair of opposite leaves having bases that completely enclose the stem so that the stem appears to pass through them.

Pergola
Horizontal timber-work or trellis supported on brick, stone or timber pillars that carries climbing plants and may form a covered walk. Originated in the Italian Renaissance becoming popular in the 19th century and developed as an architectural feature by Lutyens.

Perianth
The outer whorls of the flower. It is not concerned with reproduction but protects the reproductive organs and also acts as an attraction for insect pollinators. In angiosperms the perianth is sepals plus petals collectively.

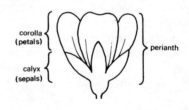

Pericycle
A plant tissue comprising the outermost layer of the root vascular tissue lying beneath the endodermis. It is where lateral roots originate in young roots. In older roots it becomes cork cambium.

Perigynous
With stamens and petals inserted on (or sometimes very near) the base of the calyx in a flower with a superior ovary.

119

Period designs
Exhibits created to reflect the atmosphere of an historical period up to the twentieth century.

Clearly defined characteristics of the Period are featured using suitable plant material, containers and accessories.

Perlite
A substance of volcanic origin which is sterile and very light, capable of high water retention but containing no nutrients. See also *Vermiculite*

Permeable
Movement of liquid substances through membranes by osmosis or diffusion. See also *Osmosis*

Perpetual
Flowering plants which produce blooms intermittently throughout their growing season (such as roses, carnations and pinks).

Persistent
Remaining attached to the plant after the normal time of withering.

Perspective
A means of depicting the three-dimensional recession of space in a two-dimensional plane and giving the visual impression of depth. Aerial perspective is produced when the atmosphere makes distant colours more blue than in the foreground, thereby giving the impression of recession.

Petal
One of the separate, often brightly coloured, leaf-like organs of a flower, whose main function is to attract pollinating insects. It also protects the stamens. A whorl of petals forms the corolla. A petal is part of the perianth.

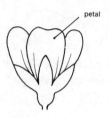

Petaloid
Applied to flower parts which resemble the shape of petals.

Petiole
The stalk of a leaf which joins it to a node on the stem.

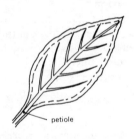

Petite
An exhibit not exceeding 230 mm in height, depth or width. This does not apply to the diagonals.

Pew-end sprays
Small arrangements designed to fit over the end of a pew for wedding ceremonies or flower festivals in church. Mechanics for these vary and care has to be taken not to damage the pews. Normally, alternate pew ends

120

are adorned this way. Such sprays are a means of carrying colour from one end of the church to the other.

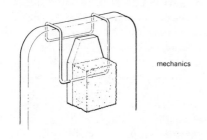

mechanics

pew-end spray

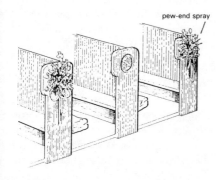

pH scale
The notation (potential of Hydrogen) which quantifies the acidity or alkalinity of soil. Certain plants will not grow in soil which is either too acid or too alkaline.

The pH range is: pH1 acid – pH7 neutral – pH14 alkaline, but soils with an acidity below pH4 and an alkalin-ity above pH9 are injurious to plants.
See also *Lime-tolerant* and *Lime-hating*

Phloem
A living tissue that conducts food materials from the leaves to other parts of the plant. It consists of hollow tubes (sieve tubes) that run parallel to the long axis of the plant organ.

Phloem contains companion cells, sieve elements and sieve plates.

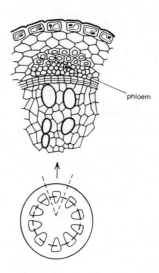

phloem

Phosphate
An inorganic mineral present in soil which is an important nutrient for plants. The notation in formulated fertilizers is P (in NPK content) P_2O_5. Phosphate assists plants to make roots and it is most in need in sandy soils. Bone meal is an organic source of phosphate.

Photoperiod
The number of hours of daylight needed by a plant before it will begin to flower.

Photosynthesis
The production of food for plants (carbohydrates), using light as a source of energy and converting carbon dioxide, water and salts. It is the conversion of simple inorganic compounds to complex organic ones.

Phototropism
The growth response of parts of

121

plants to the stimulus of light, causing them to bend at right angles towards the directional source.

See also *Geotropism*

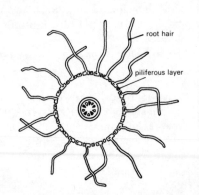

LIGHT

Phylloclade

See *Cladode*

Phyllode

Modified petiole, (leaf stalk) which looks and functions like a leaf blade. Many Acacias have such parts.

Phyllotaxis

The study of the arrangement of leaves on a stem; an important aspect of the classification of plants.

Phylum

In the classification of plants in the Plant Kingdom; another name for Divison.

Phytolaccaceae P4-5 A4-∞ G̲1-∞

Small family which includes Phytolacca – americana, the black fruit stems of which are dramatic plant material for the autumn (the seeds are poisonous).

Picotee

Petals which are narrowly edged with a band of colour; describes some Sweet Peas and Carnations.

Picture

An arrangement of fresh or preserved plant material on a background which may be framed or not, glazed or unglazed and which can be made to hang or stand.

See also *Plaque*

Picture frame

A moulding or beading fashioned to hold an oil painting, photograph or watercolour; designed to suit the subject of the picture yet not dominate the picture it encloses. It can be used as an accessory, or background in competitive work and adapted to support a container.

Picturesque

Visually pleasing or having colourful nature; graphic or vivid; originally a standard of taste in the 18th century. Developed further as an appreciation of pictorial experiences and the romantic rusticism of the late 19th century.

Pigment

(1) Natural (animal, vegetable, but chiefly mineral) or synthetic (organic or inorganic) matter which is ued to colour paints or dyes. Pigments can be either opaque or transparent, the former having 'body' to cover the surface completely.

(2) Any coloured substance present in the tissues of an organism. Pigments, like chlorophyll, are important in photosynthesis.

Piliferous layer

The layer of cells in the epidermis of the root which bears the root hairs.

root hair

piliferous layer

Pillar

A brick or stone support for a pergola; name for some types of Rose which are trained up the pillars of pergolas.

Also a tree trunk (usually section of a conifer) with stumps of branches about a foot in length left on in order to train rose climbers more easily and in a spiral manner.

Pillow

A funeral tribute (usually the more expensive type) made from a mossed wire frame, pointed at the corners, in two sections and in various sizes. Similar to cushion in technique and assembly and produced as a formal massed design.

Pilose

Covered in fine soft hairs.

Pinaceae

An enormous family of Gymnosperms comprising resinous trees with linear, awl-shaped leaves, from Abies (Silver Fir) to Tsuga (Hemlock Spruce); includes the Cypresses, Junipers, Spruces and Pines.

Pinching

The removal of small tips of growing shoots of a plant in order to promote extra side growth; to remove unwanted shoots or buds.

Pinetum

An arboretum in which evergreen conifers are grown. The National Pinetum is at Bedgebury in Kent. There are two pinetums at Nymans in Sussex, a notable one at Chatsworth House, Derbyshire and also at Stanway, Glos.

Pinholder

Lead bases in various shapes and sizes with either alloy or brass nails embedded and set closely together. They are used in containers with or without wire netting as a support for flower stems. They are not designed as an anchor for floral foam but should be protected with plastic film if used in that way. See also *Trifid*

Pink

A tint of red (white added), a 'tender' colour and 'shy' which explains the representation of femininity. It is also used to describe the highest degree of excellence or perfection.

Opt app	Psycho eff	Symb interp
light	impotent	
pale	calming	femininity
dainty	quiet	'feeling good'
gentle	kindness	

Pinnate

A compound leaf with a central axis and leaflets either side of it.

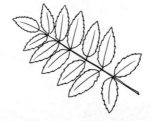

123

Pinnate (doubly)
Pinnate with each leaflet itself
pinnate.

Pinnatifid
Leaves pinnately divided into lobes
reaching more than halfway into the
midrib.

Pinning
Bending fine wire to a 'hairpin' shape
in order to secure materials to a base,
eg wreath wrap or laurel leaves to a
mossed base, or rose sepals to petals
to prevent bud opening.

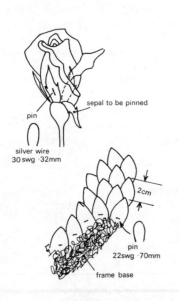

Pipped
Use of individual florets such as
Stephanotis, Hyacinth bells, etc,
wired separately in order to make up
a unit or as individual flowers in a
design.

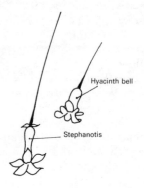

Pistil
The female reproductive organs of a
flower comprising the stigma, style
and ovary.

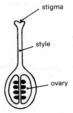

Pith
Parenchyma tissue, sometimes soft,
in the centre of stems in non-woody
dicotyledons. It is for storing food.

Pittosporaceae K5 C5 A5 $\underline{G}$(2-5)
Small family of shrubs mainly from
Australia and New Zealand not all of
which are hardy in the UK. Very
useful foliage for the florist and flower
arranger. Pittosporum is the principal member of the family of which
there are many species.

Placement
The careful positioning of an arrangement so that it is seen to its best advantage without detracting from other interesting features. In show work when two or more 'placements' are allowed (or required) then these are separate designs whether linked or not, they must be positioned carefully within the overall design.

Placenta
The part of the ovary on which the ovules are borne. The arrangement of the placenta is a very important characteristic of plant classification and identification. There are three kinds of placentation:
(1) *parietal* – in which the placentas are either situated on the outer walls or on projections from the outer walls of the ovary;
(2) *axile* – in which they are placed in the centre of two or more cells at the junction of the inner walls;
(3) *free-central* – in the centre of a one-celled ovary without any inner walls.

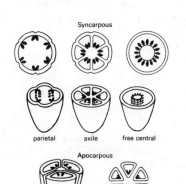

Plane
A two dimensional area bounded by an actual or imaginary line. A surface, imaginary or real, containing all the straight lines connecting any two points on it.

Plant
Any living organism of the Kingdom Plantae which has the following characteristics:
(1) possessing cell walls containing cellulose;
(2) an ability to synthesize carbohydrate by photosynthesis;
(3) a life cycle consisting of an alternation of generations;
(4) immobility (as there is no necessity to search for food).

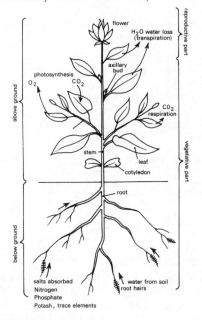

Plant kingdom
The highest category into which plant organisms are classified. Plants are arranged into related groups. The sequence in descending order is Division, Class, Order, Family.
See also *Division, Class, Order* and *Family*

Plant physiology

The functioning of organs and tissue in living plants.

Plants and Flowers

An exhibit featuring growing plants and flowers. More than one container may be used as may cut leaves and accessories.

Plaque

A design or assemblage of plant material and components in radial construction using objects that are more closely related than those used in collage. It is on a visible background, framed or not, and three dimensional in form. See also *Picture*

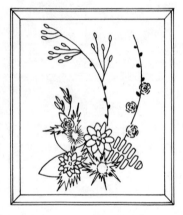

Plaster of Paris

A group of gypsum cements and a white powder that forms a paste when mixed with water and quickly hardens into a solid. Used for supporting dowelling, poles, etc, in bases or for modelling containers. Also available in a bandage form.

Plastic

The impression of space and form so that an object appears three dimensional; of mass and movement.

Plastid

The general name for the type of substances in plant cells which are surrounded by a double membrane. There are several different kinds of plastids each with a special function. See also *Chloroplasts, Chromoplasts* and *Leucoplasts*

Pleach

The weaving or interlacing of branches of closely planted trees to form a screen, eg pleached Hornbeam with serried trunks giving a colonnade effect, as at Hidcote Manor Glos.

Pleasure gardens

In earlier (Medieval) periods of English history the walled garden, which probably had a mound, was used for pleasure as well as utilitarian purposes. But from the 18th century and until the middle of the 19th century public pleasure gardens such as Vauxhall and Ranelagh (Chelsea) were established for afternoon and evening enjoyment. They were a setting for extravagant concerts, illuminations and fireworks and were quite distinct from Public parks. But by 1850 only two were left, at Royal Cremorne Gardens Chelsea and Rosherville at Gravesend. Cremorne was finally closed in 1877.

Plinth

A block or slab, generally square or rectangular, that forms the lowest part of a base of a column or pedestal; the flat base on which an object is placed.

Plumbaginaceae K(5) C(5) A(5) G(5)

Perennial herbs or shrubs which

includes Plumbago, Ceratostigma and Limonium (Statice).

Plumose
Resembling a plume, covered with small hairs such as plumose (plumate) seeds.

Plumule
The initial shoot from a germinated seed which carries the cotyledons in epigeal germination or the first foliage leaves in hypogeal germination.

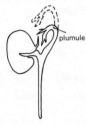

plumule

Plunge
To place clay pots (containing cuttings, plants or bulbs) up to their rims in a bed of sand or peat, etc, in order to reduce the rate of drying-out and/or to give winter protection.
See also *Plunge-bed*

Plunge-bed
A specially constructed bed with low sides (such as railway sleepers) which is filled with peat or sand in order to accommodate pots or bulbs.

Pod
A long, thin non-fleshy dry fruit, developed from a single carpel containing several seeds and which splits to disperse them when ripe.

Point
The smallest, strongest visual symbol in all designing which can balance a much larger shape. It can also be so dominant as to prevent eye move-

ment. Points can vary in shape and size but a circle holds the eye more strongly since its directional pull is inwards. In floral art terms it is one of three major shape (form) aspects of a design. Plant material has attributes of point, line or transitional forms.

Point of origin
The point at which all stems of plant material appear to originate in a design. An important requirement from a visual aspect.

Polemoniacea K(5) C(5) A5 G̲(3)
A small family of herbs – includes the climber Cobaea and such herbaceous plants as Phlox and Polemonium (Jacob's Ladder).

Pollarding
The severe lopping of branches from a tree to create new wood at its head. It has to be done regularly and is common practice with Willows.

Pollen
A mass of small grains containing the male gametes of seed plants which are produced in the pollen sacs. Pollen may be dispersed by wind or transferred by animals or insects, the latter being the more common method.

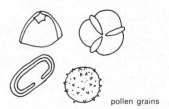

pollen grains

Pollen sac
The space inside an anther in which pollen grains are produced. There are

usually four pollen sacs in each anther in angiosperms.

t.s. of anther

Pollen tube

The outgrowth of a pollen grain which transports the male gametes to an ovule. The tube will only grow if the pollen grain has landed on the stigma and is compatible.
See also *Compatible*

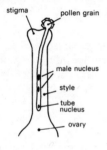

Pollination

The process by which pollen is carried from the anther to the surface of the stigma by natural or artificial means.

Pollinium

A mass of pollen grains that are carried together during pollination as the result of the adherent nature of the grains.

Polycarpic

A perennial plant, both woody and herbaceous, which is capable of producing flowers and fruit (seed) annually for several years.
See also *Monocarpic*

Polychromatic

The use of many colours together.

Polygamous

Bearing bisexual and unisexual flowers on the same plant; the condition of having these different types of flower on separate plants of the same species.

Polygonaceae P3-6 A5-8 G(3)

Small family which includes Rheum (Rhubarb), the Polygonum and Rumex genera.

Polypetalous

Having petals that are free.

Polysepalous

Having sepals that are free.

Pomander

In floristry terms 'flower ball' but strictly speaking a mixture of fragrant spices carried as a protection against infection in Tudor times when the container was made of pierced metal. Nowadays pomanders of porcelain containing potpourri are used to perfume rooms. Pomanders can be made up from oranges banded and held with ribbons and cloves inserted in the segment spaces.

Pome

A fruit in which the seeds are enclosed within a central core and surrounded by a fleshy layer. It includes apples and pears.

Pop art

A movement of the 1950s originating in Britain but which became especially fashionable in the USA. Abstract techniques were used to depict everyday objects. One feature of the art was to use 'found objects' or 'ready-mades' to make sculptures or collages with objects such as *Coca Cola* cans. Roy Lichtenstein and Andy Warhol were exponents in the USA and David Hockney among others in Britain.

Porcelain
A more or less translucent high grade of ceramic ware for which an essential ingredient is kaolin or china clay. Discovered in China in the 7th century AD it was first adopted in Europe at Dresden (Meissen factory founded 1710).

Porcelain was manufactured in England from *c* 1750 onwards. True porcelain is made from feldspar, kaoline and flint (hard paste). Soft paste is a mixture of kaolin and ground glass.

Pore
A small hole in the surface or membrane which allows a substance to pass through it.

Portique
An ornamental feature of gardens as a covered entrance either as trellis or topiary work.

Positive space
An aspect of Modern and Abstract floral art. Represented by the enclosed or partly enclosed areas with the overall design and delineated by the use of plant material, etc.
See also *Negative space*

Posterior
At the back; nearest the main axis.

Post-Impressionism
A term given to a modern French art exhibition in 1910 mounted by Roger Fry. A vague term, even today, but considered to link such painters as Cézanne, Seurat, Gauguin and Van Gogh and covering the period 1885 to 1905.

Posy bouquet
An assembly for both brides and bridesmaids; round in shape and varying in size depending on the stature of the person carrying it.

Design is made up of flowers on natural stems with false legs (or on extended legs on wired flowers) and foliage.

Victorian

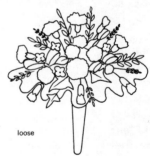
loose

Posy frill
Fabric or plastic frills which are made in several sizes and patterns for edging bridesmaid's or Victorian type posies. Some are constructed to be used for hand holders containing floral foam.

129

Posy pad

A small, informal, funeral tribute design which is round in shape, composed of suitable small and simple flowers and foliage arranged in a cylinder of floral foam secured to a plastic saucer. It is suitable for a young person to give.

Pot

A flower or plant container usually round with a narrower base than top and sloping sides. Made of clay or plastic and usually with a drainage hole if used for growing plants. Made in many sizes and square forms (in plastic).

Potash

One of the three major and essential mineral elements (K_2O) and the 'K' element of NPK fertilizer formula, contains potassium. It is found in the soil and some rocks and is most needed in sandy soils. It is the nutrient for improving the size and colour of flowers and fruits and also increases disease resistance.

Pot-bound

A plant that has completely filled its pot with roots such that little or no soil remains.

Pot et Fleur

An assemblage of growing plants, either in or out of their pots, placed in a larger receptacle which also includes a container for additional fresh cut flowers. The potted plants can be either foliage or flowering or both. In competitive work no *cut foliage* is permitted to be included in the design (other that leaves on the cut flower stems).

Pot-on

To put a plant into a larger pot in order to increase its size and make more compost/nutrients available.

Pottery

Objects and artefacts made from porous clays and fired in a kiln or dried. In earlier times they were baked. Throughout history the craft has combined utilitarian and aesthetic objectives often producing works of great beauty and decoration. Earthenware is porous unless glazed. Stoneware is fired at higher temperatures and needs no glaze.
See also *Porcelain*

Prayer book spray

An assembly, similar to a corsage, for a bride or bridesmaid who wishes to carry a prayer book. It must be in proportion to the size of the book. The flowers are attached to a ribbon which also serves as a bookmark for the marriage service.

petals) from shrivelling. The aim of pressing is to remove the water content and flatten the material without it wrinkling. Sometimes it is necessary to separate the petals from the centre of the flower to avoid this.

Prick off/prick out
To transfer seedlings from a seed tray to single stations for growing on until transplanting into pots or planting outside. Generally for bedding-out annuals.

Primary colour
The three primary colours are Red, Yellow and Blue and are the basis of the whole colour (trichromatic) pigment system. They cannot be manufactured by compounding any other colours.

Predominate
To give a component or feature greater visual emphasis than the other aspects collectively, eg a class with Roses to predominate.
See also *Dominance*

Preserving
Various ways of drying, glycerining, skeletonizing or pressing plant material so that it can be used in arrangements without the need for water and can therefore be long-lasting. Dried plant material classes imply the use of all forms of preserved plant material.

Pressed flower picture
The use of carefully selected flowers and leaves, etc, which have been pressed to preserve them and then arranged to make a design on a background which must be framed, glazed or sealed with a transparent material. A Victorian pastime, interest in which is currently being revived.

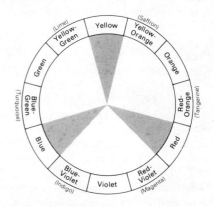

Primary growth
The thickening or increase in size of roots or shoots that occurs near the activity of the apical meristems, resulting from the expansion of the cells. See also *Secondary growth*

Pressing
A means of preserving plant material and preventing parts (leaves and

Primulaceae   K(5) C(5) A5 $\underline{G}$(5)
Fairly large family of herbs which includes Cyclamen, Primulas, Lysimachia, etc.

131

Principles of design

A universal law of the arts which, related to flower arrangement, comprises balance, scale, proportion, rhythm, contrast, dominance and harmony.

See also *Balance, Contrast, Dominance, Proportion, Rhythm* and *Scale*

Procumbent

Stems spreading near the ground.

Propagation

The process of reproduction by artificial or natural means. It can be sexual (by seed sowing) or asexual (by vegetative means).

Propagule

A part of a plant (a vegetative structure such as a bud) that becomes detached from the rest of the plant and grows into a new one.

Proportion

The correct or desirable relationship between the parts of a whole. It refers to quantity or amount – ie amount of flowers in relationship to foliage or of plant material to container, or of the whole exhibit to the space allowed. It is also the amount of light colour to dark, of rough texture to smooth, etc. The relationship of width to height. Good proportions are the essence of a good design and equal proportions usually spoils the interest and upsets unity.

Propping-up

The use of a secondary piece of wood to act as a counter prop to a large unbalanced piece of driftwood, etc.

Prostrate

Lying on the ground.

Protein

A large group of nitrogenous compounds (amino acids) that are essential constituents of all living organisms.

Protoplasm

A general name for all the living material substances and bodies inside a cell bounded by the cell membrane. All living organisms are made of protoplasm. Nucleus + cytoplasm = protoplasm. The vacuole (containing cell sap) is excluded.

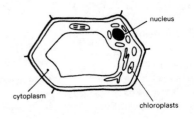

Protoplast   (energid)

All parts of a living plant cell, not including the cell wall.

Pruinose

Coated with a powdery or waxy bloom.

Pruning

The removal of unwanted growth on ornamental or fruit shrubs and trees (1) in order to regulate growth and improve shape; (2) to improve the quality of either fruit or flowers or (3) to remove diseased or damaged (including dead) wood.

Psychedelic design

A kinetic design with emphasis on the use of colourful images which heighten perception. Designs are startling. Authenticity demands distortion and violent visual action.

Psychological effect   (of colour)
The effect some colours have of stimulating the senses by implying, for example, exciting (red), or relaxing (green).
See also headings under all the individual colours, *Red, Blue, Green* etc.

Pteridophyta
A division of the Plant Kingdom comprising non-seed bearing plants which include Ferns (Filicopsida), Horsetail (Sphenopsida) and Club mosses (Lycopsida).

Pubescent
Covered with a layer of fine short hairs or down.

Public park
The first major public park was designed in 1843 by Paxton (1803-1865) for Birkenhead. He followed this with others, including a most notable one at Crystal Palace (Sydenham Hill) 1852-56. By the end of the 1860s most major cities in England had public parks.

Puddle
To dip roots of herbaceous and woody plants into a thick mixture of soil and water just before planting, in order to produce a water-holding layer of material around the roots. A Victorian practice, still favoured today.

Punctate
Having, or marked with, minute spots or depressions.

Pungent
A leaf or other feature ending in a sharp point; having an acrid smell or sharp bitter flavour.

Pure line   (Botany)
A series of generations that have identical genes for all their characteristics.

Purism
Founded by Charles Edouard Jeanneret (1887-1965), better known as Le Corbusier, in a manifesto 'After Cubism' 1918, which called upon artists to concentrate on simple geometric forms. In floral art it is the construction of a design using plant material and objects as straight lines, circles, triangles, cubes, cones, which are used as pure form.

Purple
The result of mixing the primary colours or red and blue or any hue lying between them. Includes such hues as Violet, Magenta, Mauve, Lilac, etc. It is the colour symbolizing royalty, nobility, robes of Bishops and Cardinals.

Pyramidal
Shaped like a pyramid, broad at the base and tapering to a point.

R

Raceme
A compound flower head (inflorescence) consisting of a central (sometimes pendulous) stem with numerous stalked flowers arranged regularly along it. The youngest flowers are at the top of the stem and the oldest at the base. Laburnum and Wisteria are racemes.

Racemose
Having flowers in racemes.

Rachis
The main axis or stem of an inflorescence or compound leaf.

Radial-compound
A compound leaf with leaflets radiating from a point.

Radial structure
One of the two major divisions of 20th century floral art where the area of interest (focal point) is at or near the point of emergence of the design.

Includes Modern, Traditional or free-form style design categories.

Radiation
(1) A feature of a design with an area of interest at or near a single point of emergence, with additional interest created by tapering to the edges. It is a facet of 20th century contemporary styles.
(2) Lines starting from a single point and leading in all directions.

Radicle
The part of the plant embryo that develops into a root system of the seedling and the tip of which is protected by a root cap.

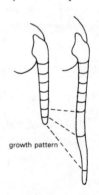

growth pattern

Raffia
The fibre obtained from the stalks of the leaves of the raffia palm (Raphia ruffia) which is used for tying stems of flowers, etc.

Ranunculaceae

P4 or more
   A ∞ G̲1∞
Large family with IV tribes which includes Clematis, Anemone, Thalictrum, Ranunculus, Paeony and Aquilegia, etc.

Ray

Horizontal, elongated, living cells radiating from the centre of the trunk of a tree. They dry out more quickly since they have a high water content and become cracks in a section of unseasoned wood.

Ray floret

A flower at the edge of a composite inflorescence which normally has a single petal (ligule).

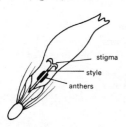

stigma
style
anthers

Receding colours

Green, violet and blue 'active' colours which appear to recede when contrasted to other colours. The use of these 'cool' colours helps to create depth in a design.
See also *Advancing colours*

Receptacle

(1) The tip of the flower stalk bearing the perianth (petals and sepals) stamens and carpels. Its development determines the position of the flower parts.

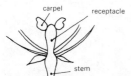

carpel
receptacle
stem

(2) Another name for container though not widely used.

Recession

The actual placement of plant materials in order to give added depth to an exhibit; clever use of colours and textures that recede and give the visual impression of depth.

Recessive

The allele that does not function when two different alleles are present in the cells of an organism.

Recurved

Petals which curve backwards from the face of the flower, eg Lilies.

Red

A primary colour which has an intense, vibrant and advancing character. It is said to increase muscular tension and stimulate higher blood pressure. Red is popular in Mediterranean societies and it is the colour associated with Communism. It is an 'aggressive' colour.
Zodiac: Aries
   Heraldry: Gules. Courage and Zeal
   effect under tungsten light: slightly orange
   effect under white fluorescent light: slightly magenta

Opt app	Psycho eff	Symb interp
fire	aggression	pride
heat	passion	vitality
radiant	loud	virility
solid	dangerous	Christmas
hard	excitement	pageantry
loud	destruction	torture
active	vigour	love
heavy	menacing	lust
	anger	desire
	courage	magic

continued...

continued

Opt app	Psycho eff	Symb interp
	friction	Socialism
	powerful	Royal livery
		fortitude
		magnanimity
		Mars

Red/orange (tangerine)
A tertiary colour obtained from the mixture of red and orange pigments;
  effect under tungsten light: brilliant red
  effect under white fluorescent light: greyish-red

Opt app	Psycho eff	Symb interp
burning	stirring	struggle
active	aggressive	revolution
restless	activating	passion
bright	spirited	power
glowing	impulsive	energy
	emotional	industriousness

Red/violet (magenta)
A tertiary colour obtained from the mixture of red and violet pigments;
  effect under tungsten light: vivid wine-red
  effect under white fluorescent light: purple/red

Opt app	Psycho eff	Symb interp
heavy	elevated	love
full	dignified	dignity
sombre	proud	wealth/opulence
	imposing	regal
	dominating	imperial
		Victorian
		temperance
		justice

Reflected colour
Reflected light distorting the surface colour of an object and affecting its hue.

Reflexed
Petals which curve sharply backwards and downwards especially chrysanthemum variety.

Regular
A flower which is symmetrical about all planes. Another name for *actinomorphic*.

Reindeer moss (or lichen moss)
A useful, but expensive, moss on which the reindeer of Lapland feed (Cladonia rangiferina). It is a good material for certain designs and is obtainable in several colours.

Remote
Leaf shape where the toothing or lobing is at the far end of the leaf.

Reniform
Having the shape or profile of a kidney.

Repetition
A means of achieving harmony in an arrangement by repeating colours, forms and textures in a rhythmical manner to give added interest to the design. Repetion must not seem fixed or mechanical. It need not be exact – merely related.

Re-pot
To transfer a plant from one pot to another of the same size (or to use the same pot after cleansing) with fresh compost or soil.

Reproduction
The process whereby organisms produce offspring like themselves, it

can be sexual or asexual and is one of the most important characteristics of living organisms.

Resin
A sticky yellow or brownish compound found in the trunks and roots of pines and other conifers. A distillate of resin yields turpentine. It is used in varnishes.

Respiration
The process whereby organisms obtain energy from the breakdown of carbohydrates. Carbon dioxide CO_2 is always a by-product. The rate of respiration dictates the longevity of plant life.

Retarding
The means of delaying the opening of flowers by keeping them in a cold-store or in some cases (Gladioli and Paeonies) by cutting them in bud and placing them flat on a stone floor, out of water.

Reticulate
The network pattern of veins of leaves. See also *parallel*

Return end
In certain wedding and funeral designs it is the placing of flowers to face back towards the tying point once the main design has been created.

Reversion
Hybrid or selected plant changing back to its prototype. Mutations which are not genetically stable may revert.

Revolute
Margins of a leaf rolled backwards and downwards.

Rhamnaceae   K4-5 C4-5 or o
   A4-5 $\underline{G}$(2-3)
Small family which includes the Ceanothus.

Rhizome
A stem, with scale leaves, which grows along at or below ground bearing buds which produce shoots. A vegetative means of reproduction because the shoots grow into whole new plants, eg Iris.

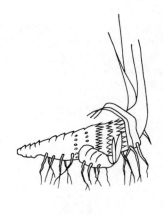

Rhomboidal

A leaf shape of rhomboid form, ie having adjacent sides of unequal length based on a parallelogram.

Rhythm

Visual activity or movement throughout a design by the repeated use of points of interest, causing the eye to travel from one to another. Repetition, gradation, radiation, transition, direction of line and visual tensions all assist in creating rhythm.

Rhythm is closely allied to dynamic balance. Rhythm is a principle of design.

Rib

A prominent vein in a leaf.

Ribbed unit

An assembly of materials either of the same kind and colour or mixed items. The materials are assembled close together graduating in size from the smallest at the tip (but with no stems of the items visible in the unit) to the largest flowers at the end.
(See also *Brancing unit*)

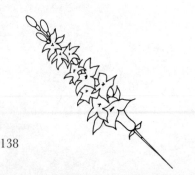

Ribbon

Narrow strips of coloured material from plain weave to highly decorative lace forms in satin, polypropylene or Lurex. An essential element of floristry sundries. It is also available in cords, braids, tubes and made-up bows.

Ripe

Fruits which are ready to release their seeds; a seed which has finished growing in the fruit; fruits which are ready to be eaten.

RNA

Ribonucleic acid occurring in all living cells and in several forms, mostly in the cytoplasm. It has an essential role in protein synthesis.

Rock garden

An area where rocks occur naturally or are introduced into a garden and in which grow plants that are specially adapted or are suitable for such terrain, eg hardy Alpine plants.
See also *Scree*

Rogue

A plant which is not true to the character of the species. Roguing is the removal of these inferior or unwanted plants.

Rond-point

The semi-circle facing the main entrance of an estate or the circle where a number of allées converge in a park or wood.

Roof garden

Although the origins of the roof garden developed from the inspiration of the Hanging Gardens of Babylon and featured in Roman and

Renaissance periods, the modern roof garden was advanced by Le Corbusier in Paris and Frank Lloyd Wright in the USA. In Britain the first major roof garden was on a department store at Derry and Toms in Kensington 1933. The concept is continually being developed world-wide.

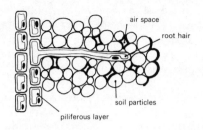

Root cap (calyptra)

A structure that is cone-shaped covering the root tip and which develops as a result of cell division by a meristem at the root apex. It protects the root tip as it grows between the soil particles.

See also *Zone of elongation, Zone of differentiation*

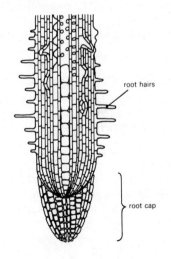

Root hairs

The main hair-like points through which water and salts are absorbed into a plant. They grow in a zone behind the root tips and are replaced as the root ages.

Root-house

A garden building constructed on a foundation of tree stumps. A Victorian feature, one example of which still survives at Badminton, Glos.

Root nodules

The swelling on the roots of the Leguminosae family in which nitrogen fixing bacteria live thus making nitrogen available to the host plant, eg Sweet Peas.

See also *Symbiosis*

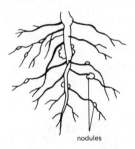

Root prune

To trim roots of lifted plants which are damaged; to cut off part of main root system of a tree in the ground to induce a more compact rooting system.

Rootstock

The roots of a plant.

Root structure

A root is a living part of a plant and

139

consists of (a) Epidermis (piliferous layer), a layer of cells without a cuticle, (b) Exodermis, the outer surface of the cortex and beneath the epidermis, (c) Cortex (parenchyma), consisting of large, thin-walled cells with air spaces between them, (d) Endodermis, which controls the passage of substances in solution into and out of the stele, (e) Casparian strip, a band of suberin preventing substances moving into the vascular cylinder from the cortex, (f) Pericycle, a layer of cells lying on the surface of the vascular cylinder (g) Vascular cylinder; tissue consisting of xylem and phloem. Xylem in roots is arranged in more or less a star-shaped pattern when seen in transverse section, and in dicotyledons there are never more than 5 groups (pentarch), sometimes 4 groups (tetrarch). In monocotyledons the roots have a large number of groups (polyarch).

See also *Zone of elongation* and *Zone of differentiation* (maturation)

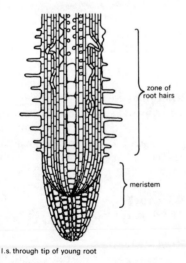

l.s. through tip of young root

Root system

The part of a vascular plant that grows down into the soil in response to gravity and the search for water. A root anchors the plant in the ground and takes up water and nutrients. Unlike stems of plants, roots do not produce nodes, leaves, buds or flowers and do not contain chlorophyll.

Roots may be developed or modified in various ways. Some are swollen to store food, eg Dahlias, others have short clasping roots for climbing, eg Ivy.

Rosaceae   K4-5 C4-5 or o
A4-∞ $\underline{G}$(1-∞)

A very large family, important chiefly for flowers and fruit; in herbaceous species the Geum, Potentilla, Alchemilla and Spiraea are included and Roses in the shrubby members.

Rot

The decay and breakdown of tissues caused by fungi or bacteria, sometimes initiated by excessive watering, mineral deficiency or by drought.

Rotate

A perianth with united petals spreading in all directions from a central point and having a very small tube or none.

Rotund

Rounded, nearly circular in shape.

Rotunda

A building having a circular shape and usually a domed roof often supported by columns in classical style. It can be open or closed.

Rounded
A leaf base which curves away regularly from the petiole.

Rounds
See *Point*

Rufous
Reddish-brown.

Rugose
Wrinkled or rough (leaves).

Ruin
The Gothic ruin became a fashion of English gardening in the late 18th century often to give a touch of romance to the scene. A ruined arch at Kew still survives.

Runcinate
Having a saw-toothed margin with the lobes or teeth pointing backwards.

Runner
An horizontal stem growing along the surface of the ground and which produces shoots from axillary buds which root, the process being repeated. Strawberry and Creeping Buttercup are examples.

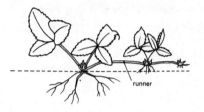

runner

Rust
Parasitic fungus infecting a number of plants causing red and black spots on leaves stems and some fruits.

Rutaceae K4-5 or (4-5)
   C4-5 A8-15 G(2-5)
Small family of aromatic herbs which includes Dictamnus, Ruta graveolens and Choisya ternata.

S

Saccate
In the form of a sac or pouch which is not pronounced enough to be termed a *spur*.

Sagittate
A leaf shape in the manner of an arrow-head.

St Valentine's Day
February 14th and a significant day marked by the gift of red roses or other tokens of love. Associated with the Roman festival of Lupercalia, a festival of fertility, or with the mating season of birds. It is considered to be the day for choosing a sweetheart and sending cards with cryptic messages of love. In the Old English table of flowers, the early primrose and crocus were associated with the day.

Salicaceae   Po A2-30 G̲(2)
The large Poplar and Willow family.

Samara
A small, dry, single-seeded, achene or fruit capable of being dispersed by the wind – such as the Sycamore and Ash which have 'wings', the Sycamore being a double samara.

142

Sap
Water and nutrients contained and transported in the xylem and phloem of plants; a term generally used for any liquid (such as latex) exuded by plants.

Sap wood
One section of the major part of a thickened stem which surrounds the heart wood, and is lighter in colour. Water and dissolved food materials pass through it to the rest of the trunk or branch.

Saprophyte
A plant that absorbs nutrients from dead organic matter such as fungi and bacteria. It is important in the 'food chain', bringing about decay and release of nutrients for plant growth.

Saturation or value   (of colour)
The lightness or darkness of hues; colour can be described as being tinted – mixed with white or toned-mixed with grey, or shaded – mixed with black. See also *Colour intensity*

Saut de loup

A deep trench which is dug at the end of an allée in order to prevent trespass or the entry of animals; the equivalent of a *ha-ha*.

Saxifragaceae K4-5 C5-5 or o A8-10 G2-5 or (2-5)

A diverse family of plants which includes all the many Saxifraga as well as Tellima, Heuchera, Tiarella, Astilbe and Rodgersia. Included in the shrub section are Deutzia, Escallonia, Hydrangea, Philadelphus (Mock Orange) and Ribes.

Scabrous

Rough to the touch because of small projections.

Scale

The relative size of one part or component to another – the size of an accessory to the exhibit, the size of the container to the height of the design, the size of the smallest flower compared with the largest. Scale is a principle of design.

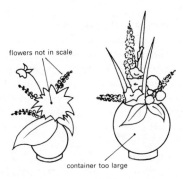

flowers not in scale

container too large

Scale (botany)

A minute leaf, bract or an outgrowth on the surface of a leaf or shoot, especially the protective covering of a bud.

Scale scars

The scars formed as the result of bud scales falling from a twig after the bud has opened in the spring. They form a ring around the stem and indicate annual growth of a twig.

Scandent

Plants that have a climbing habit.

Scape

A leafless flower stalk arising from a rosette of leaves growing from the level of the ground.

Scarify

Mechanical scratching or breaking of seed coats in order to make them permeable to water prior to germination.

Scarious

Parts of plants that are membranous, dry and brownish in colour.

Schedule

A complete list of requirements, viz details of dates, times, venue, instructions and wording for various classes in a show and which gives conditions and measurements with which competitors must comply. Failure to comply with all conditions results in disqualification, termed *not according to schedule*.

Schizocarp

A fruit which splits into separate one-seeded portions when mature.

Scion

A bud or shoot removed from a parent plant for budding or grafting on to other stock.

143

Sclerenchyma

Hard, lignified tissue, impervious to oxygen, giving mechanical strength to stems and roots, its function being support.

Scorpioid

A cymose inflorescence having the main stem coiled before development, as in Boraginaceae.

Scree-garden

A small-scale duplication of weathered rock fragments making a sloping heap as at the foot of a cliff. Another term for *moraine*.

Screen

A wall, fence or hedge that encloses a garden, baffles the wind, or hides an ugly view.

Scroll

Curving or spiralling ornamentation in carving or moulding resembling a roll of parchment.

Scrophulariaceae   K(5) C(5) A2-5 G̲(2)

Large family (IX tribes) which includes Verbascum, Calceolaria, Antirrhinum, Pentstemon, Digitalis and Veronica (Hebe).

Sculpture

The creation of a form in three dimensions by carving, assembling or modelling in many mediums and materials.

Sea fan   (coral)

Any of the various corals (marine invertebrates) of the genus Gorgonia having a tree-like or fan-shaped horny skeleton. Common in tropical seas. An accessory in competitive work.

Seaweed

Multicellular marine algae that grows on the seashore, salt marshes, etc, and is natural plant material.

Secondary colours

The three secondary colours are exact intermediates between the primary colours and are made by mixing equal quantities of any two primary colours.

Red + Yellow = Orange
Red + Blue = Violet
Blue + Yellow = Green

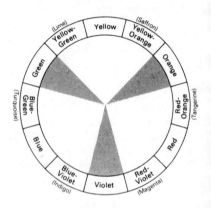

Secondary thickening

The thickening of a stem or a root due to the activities of vascular and cork cambium which gives the plant extra support. Secondary thickening occurs in most dicotyledons and gymnosperms but never in monocotyledons.

Secretion

The dissolved liquid produced and exuded by a cell or organ.

Seed

The fertilized ripe ovule in angiosperms and gymnosperms. The seed is covered by a protective layer (testa) and contains the embryo and endosperm. Angiosperm seeds are contained within a fruit. Those of gymnosperms lack an enclosing fruit and are produced in cones and are termed *naked*.

Seed-heads
The mature, fertilized seeds of an inflorescence which are often very decorative and may be used as flowers or fruit at any stage of their development in competitive work.

Seed leaf
See *Cotyledon*

Seed pans
Shallow plastic or clay round pots which are about half their diameter in depth used for seed sowing.

Seedling
A young plant with a single, soft and unbranched stem which has been grown from a seed.

Seeing eye
The all important ability of noticing how nature works, how pictures were painted, the organization of design elements and principles, the periods of history especially related to floral art; the value of perception and the training to observe.

Self-coloured
A flower of a single colour, eg self-carnations having one colour only, as compared with fancies having more than one colour.

Self-fertilization
The fertilization of a female gamete by a male gamete from the same plant. Sometimes called *selfing*.

Self-pollination
The pollination of an ovule by pollen from the same flower or another flower on the same plant.

Self-sterile
An individual plant which cannot fertilize itself and needs a pollinating partner to produce seed and fruit. Also termed *self-incompatible*.

Segregation, Law of
Mendel's first Law which states that certain paired characteristics (alleles), one from each parent, do not blend with or alter each other in the offspring. This accounts for contrasting traits in successive generations.

Semi-crescent bouquet
A formal type bouquet design based on less than one third of the arc of a circle with natural or wired flowers and foliage. The design can curve to the right or left but should be emphasized both at the trailing and return end.

Semi-double
Flowers with more than the normal number of petals, but with the centre still comprising stamens and pistil, etc. See also *Double*

Semi-evergreen
Shrubs and trees that are normally evergreen but lose some or all of their leaves in a severe winter.

Semi-internal wiring
A method of wiring for 'difficult' flowers with hard stems, where the wire is inserted below the flowerhead into the seedbox and the rest of the wire is taped and then blended with the stem.

Senescence
The changes and process that occur in an organism (or part) between maturity and death, ie the process of ageing.

Sepal
That part of a flower which makes up the calyx and is the outer layer of the flower bud. Sepals are usually green and sometimes have hairs.

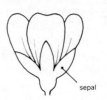
sepal

Sepia
A brown pigment obtained from the ink secretion of the cuttlefish and octopus. Used by the Romans and popularized in the early 19th century. The pigment tends to fade in strong sunlight.

Septum
A dividing partition between two tissues.

Serpentine wall
A wall, usually running east to west, built of brick in curving lines, in order to reflect the sun's rays and ripen the fruit against which the trees were grown. An economical method of wall construction. Sometimes with added coping of tiles and straw. Also known as a *crinkle-crankle wall*.

Serrate
A leaf margin where the edge is saw-toothed.

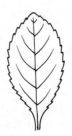

Serrulate
Minutely serrate.

Sessile
An organ without a stalk, eg leaves without petioles or flowers without pedicels, attached directly to the stem.

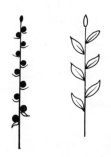

Set
(1) Certain bulbs and tubers which are planted out early in the season.
(2) Blossom or flowers are said to have set when they have been fertilized and the fruit has started to form.

Setose
Covered with bristles.

Settings
(1) The background or surroundings against which an arrangement or exhibit is placed so that the style and setting harmonize. A design is enhanced still more if its setting is both beautiful and compatible.

(2) Place settings are the integrated use of cutlery, wine glasses, napkins, table mats, etc, for a formal luncheon or dinner table.

Sexual reproduction
The fusion of two cells and their nuclei from two parents so that the offspring receives genetic material from both. Sexual reproduction occurs in all divisions of the plant kingdom.

Sfumato
Italian word describing a gradual transition between areas of different colour avoiding sharp outlines; shaded off.

Shade (of colour)
(1) Any spectrum colour darkened by the addition of black.
(2) The dark area of an object or exhibit as a result of the obstruction of a light-source.

Shade
(1) To cover plants (particularly cuttings and seedlings) from direct sunlight by various means in order to avoid scorching or stress.
(2) The natural cover given by over-head foliage on trees. Its density determines what type of plant will be most suitable to underplant.

Shape
The outward form of anything as defined by an outline, eg round shape, square shape, pear-shaped, etc.

Sheaf
A funeral design that can be made as a natural bunch with a return end of stalks or a rounded end with flowers.

147

The design has a focal area and depth created by the elevation of certain larger flowers at the focal point.

Sheath
A tubular protective covering or envelope such as the lower part of a grass leaf.

Shells
The hard outer covering of molluscs used as accessories in competitive work.

Shell-work
The use of shells to embellish the façades of grottoes or follies either in patterns or random placings. Popular in Europe in the 18th century and continued into the 19th century. Used to decorate artefacts as well as making bouquets from petalled flowers which were often mounted and covered by a glass dome.

Shelter-belt
A single or several rows of trees planted to create a windbreak; best suited to large gardens exposed to strong winds.

Shoot
A stem of a plant which is one year old or less.

Shoot system
The organs of a typical flowering plant which grows above the soil.

Shower bouquet   (also called classic bouquet)
A symmetrical design with a rounded outline at the top tapering down to the tail, the widest part being at the focal point. The flowers may be mixed or a single variety of flower.

Shrub
A plant with woody steams and branches but with no central trunk and varying in height considerably. Shrubs may be evergreen or deciduous.

Side-shoot
See *Lateral*

Sieve element
Long, thin plant cells occuring within the phloem which combine to form a series of tubes connecting leaves, shoots and roots and through which food materials are transported via sieve plates.

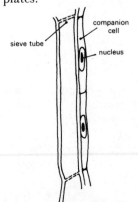

Sieve plate
The perforated ends of a sieve element through which dissolved food can pass to other parts of the plant.

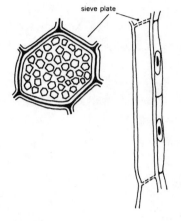

Sieve tube
A long tube within the phloem tissue of a plant composed of joined sieve elements.

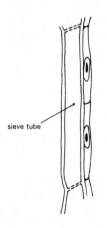

Significant form
An aesthetic term describing the visual arts whereby the arrangement of form, line and colour determines and identifies the piece as art.

Silhouette
A representation of the outline of a shape, usually as a black image on a background; the outline of a solid object as cast by its shadow.

Silica gel
An amorphous (lacking shape) silica that resembles white sand and is used as a drying and de-humidifying agent in preserving plant materials, especially flower heads.
See also *Desiccant*

Silicula
A long dry fruit developed from an ovary consisting of two carpels. It is flat longitudinally and divided into two cavities. An example is the family Cruciferae (Iberis). See also *Siliqua*

Siliqua
A long dry fruit developed from an ovary consisting of two carpels; resembles silicula but is longer than broad. Examples are the family Cruciferae (Cheiranthus cheiri).

Simple
Leaves which are not divided into leaflets and consist of a single, solid blade.

Simplicity
The hallmark of distinction characterized by fewer forms, purer art, and stronger message. Emphasis or dominance is a pre-requisite. A haphazard selection of materials has to be avoided to achieve simplicity.

Simultaneous contrast
The way in which two colours act upon each other, ie the mutually intensifying nature of complementary colours; the effect of placing neutral

grey alongside a strong colour when the grey appears to be tinged with the complementary colour.

Singeing
A method of conditioning stems that exude a latex from cuts. Singeing seals the ends and kills the cells to prevent bleeding. The heat also chars the rubbery material so that it is no longer impermeable to water. This type of conditioning is necessary for Euphorbias, Poppies and Helleborus foetidus, etc.

Single
A flower with the normal number of petals.

Single-leg mount
The addition of a wire to the base of a stem of a flower or foliage for anchorage in such a way that only one wire protrudes from the stem. The shorter wire must not extend past the base of the natural stem.
See also *Double-leg mount*

Sinuate
Leaves having a strongly waved margin.

Sinus
Small rounded notch between two lobes or divisions of a leaf, petal, etc.

Skeletonizing
Removal of cellular plant tissue from leaves so that only the veins remain. It is a means of preserving mature (but not old) leaves such as Magnolia, Ivy, Laurel, etc.

Slip
A cutting obtained by pulling a side-shoot away from the main stem and propagating as for a stem cutting.

Snag
The torn stub of a shoot or branch which is left after bad pruning. It will die back allowing disease to enter.

Soil profile
The arrangement of different layers of material in the soil in horizontal layers. The top layers are usually organic and the lower ones inorganic.

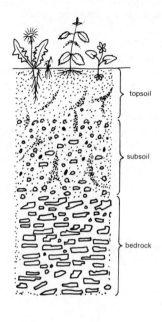

topsoil

subsoil

bedrock

'heavy' and retentive of moisture. See also *Soil structure*.

Solanaceae K(5) C(5) A5 G̲ (2)
Family including the potato and tomato as well as Salpiglossus, Petunia, Nicotiana and Schizanthus.

Solitary
Organs borne singly; a single flower at the end of a stem; a bud found in the axil.

Soluble
Substances which can be dissolved in liquids.

Solution
A liquid with substances dissolved in it.

Solvent
A liquid or substance capable of dissolving another substance.

Space
The three-dimensional expanse into which a design is placed. The space enhances the form.

The use of space is an important aspect of Abstract and Modern designs where enclosed space is considered as important as the solid forms. It can thus be the most dominant feature of the design. In traditional mass designs, voids are limited to the outer boundaries of the design.
See also *Negative space* and *Positive space*

Spadix
A column-like type of flowering spike with a large fleshy floral axis with many small sessile flowers. These are usually unisexual as in the

Soil structure
Refers to the arrangement of soil particles into larger aggregates – the way they are grouped. In sandy soil the grains are not joined. When clay and humus are present they bind soil particles into aggregates which vary from crumbs to large clods. A crumb structure is friable soil with a good tilth.

Soil texture
Soils are commonly classified as sands, silts or clays and the proportion determines the texture:
light soils – sand and sandy loam;
medium soils – loam and silt loam;
heavy soils – clay and clay loam.
Where coarse particles predominate the soil is described 'light' and freely draining, if minute it is described as

151

Anthurium or Arum lily. The spadix is surrounded by a spathe. See also *Spathe*

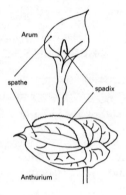

Spathe
(1) The single large petal-like bract (modified leaf) surrounding the spadix in such flowers as Anthurium, Arum lily, etc.
(2) The woody bract from the coco-nut palm tree, often curved, with a cross-section which is saucer-like in form.

Spathulate
A simple leaf-shape having a narrow base and a broad, rounded apex.

Species
The smallest unit of classification of plants in the Plant Kingdom. Species are part of binomial nomenclature and can be divided into sub-species and varieties for some plants.

Specimen plant
A plant, shrub or tree that is positioned in a prominent position so that it may be seen from all angles.

Spectrum
The distribution of colours produced when white light is dispersed by a prism. The visible range is blue-violet to red. Seven colours are normally distinguished in the spectrum: Violet, Indigo, Blue, Green, Yellow, Orange and Red.

Spermatophyte
A plant of the divison Spermatophyta which includes all seed-bearing plants of gymnosperms and angio-sperms.

Sphagnum moss
Any moss of the sub-class Sphagnidae (genus Sphagnum) grown in temperate bogs, layers of which decayed to form peat.
See also *Peat*

Spicate
Relating to spikes such as infloresc-ences having, or being arranged in spikes.

Spices
Any of the variety of aromatic vegetable substances which came originally from oriental tropical regions, mostly from trees or shrubs. They are used as flavourings.

Spike
A compound inflorescence consisting of a central stem along which are

arranged numerous stalkless (sessile) florets (such as Gladiolus).

Spine
The sharply pointed tip of a leaf or stem which is outgrowing such as Ilex aquifolium 'Ferox' (Hedgehog Holly).

Spit
One spade's depth of soil, a term used in cultivating or digging.

Split complementary colour
A contrasting harmony of three hues, comprising BOTH colours either side of the true complementary, eg
(a) Blue: Yellow/orange and Red/orange
(b) Blue/green: Orange and Red.

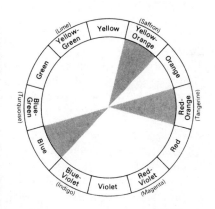

Spongy mesophyll
A tissue comprising irregularly shaped cells and large air spaces beneath the pallisade layer in the leaves of many plants.

Spore
An asexual reproductive organ (usually single celled), characteristic of non-flowering plants such as mosses, ferns or fungi.

Sport
A flower colour different from the parent plant especially with chrysanthemums.

Spray
See *Corsage*

Spraying
(1) The application of a fine mist of water once an exhibit has been staged in order to reduce transpiration of the plant material. (2) The colouring of plant material by aerosol sprays where this is permitted in show schedules.

Sprout
A young shoot, especially that growing on a tuber or germinating seed.

Spur
(1) A tubular extension at the base of the corolla in some flowers such as Aquilegia, Delphinium, etc.
(2) A short, stiff, small branch such as a fruiting spur on top fruit trees.

Stabile
An exhibit expressing arrested, or imminent, motion or appearing to move. Can be designed with any combination of plant materials with

153

accessories. It is inspired by sculpture and was devised and named by Alexander Calder. The container and/or accessories sometimes form the dominant feature and carry the interpretation.

See also *Mobile, Stamobile*

Stamen

The male reproductive organ of a flower, consisting of the pollen-bearing anther at one end of the filament. See also *Androecium*

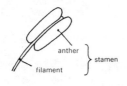

Staminate

Flowers which have stamens but no carpels.

Staminode

A sterile stamen which does not produce pollen, or a structure like a stamen.

Stamobile

A contraction of stabile and mobile. A design to which an extension has been added which actually moves, ie a stabile arrangement (implied movement) with a mobile which creates added interest. The mobile part may be actually attached to the stabile or be suspended in juxtaposition, but it must join the stabile visually to form an integrated design.

Standard

(1) One of the upright petals of the bearded iris.

(2) A type of rose plant where the variety is grafted on to the top of a tall stem of briar stock.

(3) Tree with a bare trunk several feet tall before the first branching occurs.

Starch

A polymer of two glucoses, the carbohydrate of which is produced by photosynthesis and stored in plants as a source of energy.

Starting

Encouraging dormant plants into growth, usually for tuberous subjects such as Begonias and Gloxinias. They are placed in a mixture of peat and sand in warmth and moist conditions until roots and shoots are formed, after which they are potted on.

Static balance

An aspect of both Symmetrical and Asymmetrical designs achieved by actual or visual weight exerting equal force in opposing directions. There is less attraction and no rhythm or movement in a design with static balance.

Station-sowing

The practice of sowing seeds at the appropriate distance at which they are to grow without being thinned out or transplanted.

Statuary

An important feature in the gardens of ancient Greece and Rome and revived in 16th century Italy and 17th century France. Still part of garden ornament and now includes modern sculpture which is best suited to a contemporary setting.

Stellate
Resembling a star in shape or radiating from the centre such as an arrangement of petals.

Stem
The central part of most plants on which there are nodes and buds and from which leaves and flowers grow. The stem conducts water and minerals from the roots and distributes food produced in the leaves to other parts of the plant. Most stems are above ground but are sometimes modified for other purposes and grow underground (rhizomes).
See also *Rhizomes*

Stem cutting, hardwood
A cutting prepared from the mature wood of trees or shrubs in the autumn and winter, after leaf fall.

Stem cutting, heel
Semi-ripe or hard-wood cutting, torn from an older shoot with a small piece of older wood at its base. Too many cuttings of this type should not be taken from a mother plant at any one time. The heel is trimmed before inserting in the rooting medium.

Stem cutting, internodal
A cutting prepared by severing a shoot midway between two nodes.

Stem cutting, nodal
A cutting prepared from the shoot of a tree or shrub immediately below a node.

Stem cutting, soft-wood
A cutting prepared from a young

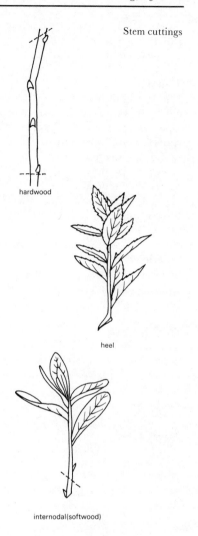

Stem cuttings

hardwood

heel

internodal(softwood)

nodal

shoot which is still extending in growth. It is therefore taken early in the season with leaves attached.

Stencil
A pattern cut into thick vellum-type paper or other rigid surface as an 'open window' mask. Paint or ink is spread or dabbled across the stencil so that an image is formed. Beautiful examples of flowers and fruit, etc, stencilled on furniture and walls were created in America in the 19th century, especially in New England and Pennsylvania.

Sterile
Organisms which cannot produce offspring, or plants incapable of producing seed, fruit or spores.

Sterilization
The treatment of soil either in the greenhouse or garden in order to destroy weed seeds, bacteria or fungi. Soil can be sterilized by steam, heat or chemical means.

Stigma
The tip of the style (part of the female reproductive organ) of a flower. It receives pollen on the sticky surface once ovules are ready for fertilization.

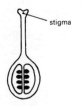

stigma

Still life
A composition with plant material (fresh or preserved) to which inanimate objects, furnishings, etc,

are grouped to create an overall design with a unified aesthetic appeal. Its charm lies in the theme interpreted more by the objects used than the plant material with a varying relationship of line, form, textures and colour. Plant material must always predominate.

Stipe
A stalk in plants that bears reproductive structures, such as a mushroom.

Stipitate
Stalked, possessing a stripe or borne on the end of stalk bearing reproductive structures.

Stipule
A small outgrowth from the leaf-base (petiole) found in many plants, sometimes protecting an axillary bud.

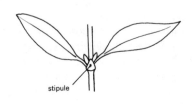

stipule

Stitching
The wire support for leaves, which can be executed in several ways according to the type of leaf. Some leaves can be wire-stitched with a small horizontal loop through the main vein about one third of the way from the apex or tip of the leaf, the ends of the wire being brought down to the base for mounting. Long leaves need several stitches from stem to tip

of leaf, with the shorter sections of wire showing on the front side of the leaf.

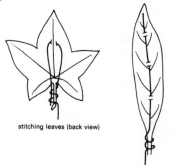

stitching leaves (back view)

Stolon

A long stem which arches towards the ground and its tip produces adventitious roots when it touches the surface, such as Blackberry.

stolon

Stoma   (plural = stomata)

A pore in the epidermis of leaves mostly on the under surface (except on aquatic plants), bordered by two guard cells which open and close thus controlling the size of the aperture allowing water to evaporate and CO_2 to enter.

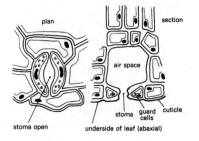

plan   section

air space

stoma guard cuticle
cells

stoma open   underside of leaf (abaxial)

Stone trough

A natural or fabricated container in which to grow suitable plants for Spring and Summer seasons, but more particularly in which to grow alpine plants. The troughs can be raised to afford closer inspection and easy maintenance.

Stones

Considered as natural mineral objects and accessories in competitive work. May be used as a base in some interpretative exhibits especially flat stones.

Stool

(1) The base of a bushy plant producing shoots from ground level or above, eg Chrysanthemum

(2) A plant is cut to the ground annually in Feb/March for production of new shoots which are earthed up to encourage rooting. It is a method of vegetative reproduction for rootstocks.

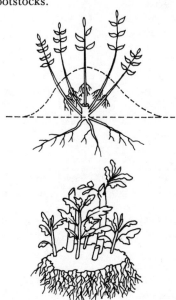

Stop

To remove the growing-point in order to induce branching or breaks from side shoots.

Strain

The characteristics of a group of organisms within a species; variations in a plant which have been isolated over many generations in breeding and selected by Seedsmen in order to raise or breed new varieties.

Stratification

Storing seeds in moist sand for a period, often at low temperatures, to induce completion of the after-ripening and thereafter the decomposition of fruit and seed coat to promote germination.

Striated

Marked with fine vertical lines, eg leaf veins.

Strigose

Bearing, or clothed with, fine stiff hairs or bristles.

Strike

The induction of roots at the base of stem cuttings by creating the necessary conditions. The cuttings are said to have 'struck' once roots are produced.

Stripping

(1) The removal of bark from wood to reveal the smoother texture of the stem or root.
(2) The removal of thorns from the stems of roses.

Structure

The arrangement of parts of a plant, ie tissues, cells and organs with a definite form or purpose, eg leaf structure.

Style

A distinctive formal or characteristic manner of expression, elegance or refinement in works of art or cultural trends.

In flower arrangement, style is design in historical periods, or changes within an historical period, especially in twentieth century, viz Geometric style, Abstract, Modern, etc.

Style (botany)

The long slender extension of the ovary bearing the stigma. After pollen has reached the stigma the pollen tubes grow through the style to the ovary in order for fertilization to occur.

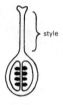

Suberin

A mixture of waxy or fatty substances which is present in the cork tissues of trees and shrubs and which prevents water from entering through the cork. It also makes tissues resistant to decay.

Sub-opposite

Nearly, but not quite opposite.

Sub-shrub

An intermediate between an herbaceous plant and a shrub, producing some woody growth at the base; the top growth dies back annually.

Subsoil
The lower inorganic horizon of a soil profile containing minerals from weathered parent rock.
See also *Soil profile* and *Topsoil*

Subulate
Tapering to a point or awl-shaped.

Succession
The series of changes which occur naturally, such as one type of vegetation changing to another.

Successive contrast
See *Accidental colour*

Succulent
A plant that conserves water by means of water-storing tissues in the thick fleshy leaves and stems. In competitive floral art classes it is not obligatory to have succulents (such as Sempervivums) or cacti in water or water-retaining material.

Sucker
A shoot that rises from an underground root or stem and grows at the expense of the parent plant. It is a means of vegetative reproduction (propagation). Where the suckers originate from the rootstock of a

grafted plant they should be removed, otherwise vigour is lost to the graft.

Sugar
A carbohydrate, produced by photosynthesis and soluble in water.
See also *Photosynthesis*

Sulphur
A chemical used as a fungicide and acaricide (killing mites or ticks). Cut surfaces of tubers, corms, etc, can be dusted with green sulphur to prevent rotting.

Superior
A structure that is positioned above or higher than another structure, eg superior ovary means that it is positioned above the other organs of the flower (the stamens and perianth). See also *Inferior*

Superphosphate
The oldest artificial fertilizer, patented in 1842 by Sir J B Lawes; it is the main phosphorous fertilizer of most countries. Phosphates are the major plant nutrient for making roots.

Superstition
Some flowers and colour associations are considered to be unlucky and should be avoided, especially red and white for hospital patients.

Suprematism
A Russian movement founded by Malevich in 1915 the basis of which was an abstract style using the circle, rectangle, triangle and cross as simple geometric form.

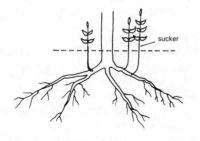

sucker

159

Support wiring

The use of the finest gauge wire possible in order to achieve the necessary strength and control of flower materials but where the wiring finishes at the stem end of the material.

See also *Internal wiring, External wiring* and *Stitching*

Surrealism

Originally an offshoot of Dada it emerged in Paris in the 1920s as a literary movement. Surrealist art (super reality) comprises on the one hand detailed, fantastic, imagined landscapes and dream worlds with distorted images as in the work of Salvador Dali and on the other, frottages and collages representing the results of unconscious mental processes exemplified by Max Ernst and Jean Arp. See also *Dada*

For interpretative floral art the theme depicts contexts and juxtapositions impossible in nature. Surrealism attempts to portray dreams and nightmares, which are weird and sinister.

Suture

A line marking the point of dehiscence in a seed pod or capsule; the line of junction of two carpels.

Swag

An assemblage of fresh or preserved plant material, with or without accessories, loose, or on a background which is *not* visible. It is a three dimensional design. In some cases it represents the concept of wood carvings in the manner of those of Grinling Gibbons (1648-1721).

SWG

Abbreviation for Standard Wire Gauge, ie the notation of the diameter of the various wire thicknesses; now superseded by the use of metric measurements and equivalents.

See also *Wire*

Symbiosis

Individual organisms of different species that live closely together or interact for much of their lives, such as lichen which is an obligatory symbiotic relationship between algae and fungi.

Symbolic colour

The communication of colours which represent interpretation of moods:

Black – sorrow

White – innocence, purity, youth

Red – aggressive, danger, stimulating, exciting

Yellow – sunshine, energy, cheerfulness

160

Blue – dignity, formality
Orange – caution, excitement
Green – eternity, rebirth
Violet – dignity, royalty
Browns and *low key colours* – stability,
Grey – humility
Pink, lavender and *pastel shades* –
   femininity, gentleness
See also under individual colour
headings for additional keys

Symbolic interpretation (of colour)

Association of colours with seasons,
months, anniversaries and festivals,
etc eg *Church Festivals:*
Christmas – Crimson, red and green
Easter – Gold, mauve and bright green
Harvest – Autumnal colours – brown
   reddish-brown, etc.
See also *Symbolic Interpretation* under
headings of *Red, Blue, Yellow, etc.*

Symbolism

Used in connection with flowers and
plants for centuries as with insects
and birds, etc; the 'Vanitas' in
Flemish flower paintings. Also used
in the language of flowers in
Victorian times, some symbolism of
which still persists today.

   Types of plant material can also be
used and placed in such a manner as
to imply some representation of
symbolism.

Symmetrical (botany)

Describes flower structures whose
parts are arranged equally and
regularly on either side of a line (or
plane) as zygomorphic flower
(bilateral symmetry) or actinomorphic (radially symmetrical).
See also *Actinomorphic* and *Zygomorphic*

Symmetrical balance

Visual stability obtained by use of
regular, equal amounts of plant
material on either side of an
imaginary central axis. The central
axis is stressed. Symmetrically
balanced designs are most often
associated with Period Occidental or
Formal Designs giving static and
perfect equilibrium.

Symmetry

The exact correspondence in position
or form about a given point, line or
plane; a mirror image either side of a
vertical or horizontal axis.
See also *Symmetrical balance*

Sympathy basket

An arrangement of flowers in a basket
with a carrying handle. The whole
design should be attractive when
viewed from any angle and can be
arranged in a linear manner, with
flowers either side of the handle as a
focal point and can be finished with a
ribbon to one side.

161

Sympodial

The type of growth of a plant in which the lateral buds near the apex grow and the growth from the apex ceases. See also *Dichotomous* and *Monopodial*

Syncarpous

The structure whereby the carpels (female reproductive organs) are joined to each other, as for example the Liliaceae. It is an important characteristic in the plant classification of angiosperms.
See also *Apocarpus*

Systemic

Spreading throughout the plant, eg insecticide which when sprayed on a plant is absorbed by it and then renders the sap toxic to sap-sucking insects.

T

Table decoration (table centre)
An arrangement for a suitable occasion such as luncheon, dinner, or buffet, with style and degree of formality to match.

Any plant material used should avoid overpowering or unpleasant smelling flowers or foliage. Competitive exhibits for luncheon and dinner occasions are judged in both standing and seated positions.

A guest should not be prevented from holding a conversation across the table by large arrangements which obscure the guest opposite.

Tactile
Namely texture value, rough or smooth, which can be assessed by touch, as opposed to visual quality of texture. See also *Texture*

Tannin
Yellow-brown solid compounds found in the bark, wood and other parts of plants used in tanning hides for leathers and as medical astringents.

Taping
The use of various makes (both in colours and types) of tape (such as gutta percha) for covering and concealing wiring in floristry work; for securing mechanics and floral foam to containers.

The taping of short wired flower and leaf stems helps to seal the stem thus preventing excess moisture loss. For finer work the tape width can be split in two.

Tapis vert
Grass cut in regular shape; a feature of French 17th century gardens (literally 'green cloth').

Tap root
The main, long, anchoring and primary root of a plant which is much thicker than its lateral roots. It acts as a source of food for the plant and is in some cases edible (carrot, parsnip, etc).

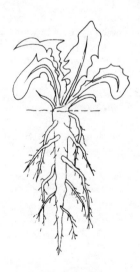

Taxon (Pural = taxa)
A unit in taxonomic terms for categories such as family, genus, species or variety according to the observed similarities of the structure of plants. See also *Taxonomy*

Taxonomy
The attribution of the correct botanical name to each plant. It is related to classification, being the relationships among the species.

Technique
Proficiency in practical method; skill or art in floristry or flower arranging.

Temple
A feature in large gardens in the 18th and 19th centuries and forming a focal point with associated planting. Built in stone of classical design and dedicated to a variety of patrons, eg Temple of Venus, Temple of Ancient Virtue.

Tender
Plants which are liable to frost damage when grown outdoors; very young plants before they have become established or hardened-off.

Tendril
Thin, stem-like and curling outgrowth arising from the stem or leaf stalk of such plants as Sweet Pea, Clematis, etc.

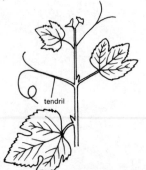

tendril

Tepals
Collective term for petals and sepals (floral leaves) which are so similar that they are indistinguishable. They are characteristic of many monocotyledon flowers, are often called perianth segments and are usually six in number – either separate or fused together.

Terete
Plant-parts which are circular in section and tapering.

Terminal bud
The shoot or bud at the end of the growth extension of a plant, as opposed to lateral bud.

Ternate
(1) A leaf consisting of three leaflets
(2) Plants having three groups of members.

Terrace
A horizontal flat area of ground, generally one of a series in a slope. Originated in Egypt, featured in classical Roman times and a tradition carried through the Middle Ages, Italian Renaissance to the Italianate gardens of the Victorian period.

Terra cotta
A hard, fired, unglazed clay, usually brownish-red in colour used since the Neolithic age for simple pots, figurines, tiles, etc.

Terrarium
A glass container often made in the form of a miniature hexagonal greenhouse in which suitable plants can be grown. Two sides are left open for planting and management.
See also *Bottle-garden*

Tertiary colour

Any of six colours obtained by mixing a primary colour with the secondary colour nearest to it.

Red + Violet = Red/violet (Magenta)

Blue + Violet = Blue/violet (Indigo)

Blue + Green = Blue/green (Turquoise)

Yellow + Green = Yellow/green (Lime)

Yellow + Orange = Yellow/orange (Saffron)

Red + Orange = Red/orange (Tangerine)

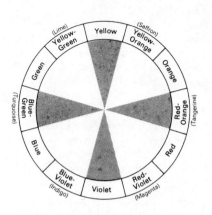

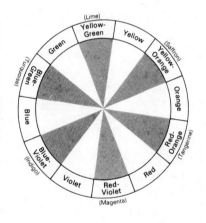

Testa

The seed coat which is a hard, protective, outer layer, covering the embryo. It prevents water entering and rotting the seed before germination.

Tetradic colour

A four colour harmony made up from four colours at equal distances around the colour circle (every third segment). They are contrasting harmonies of four hues.

Tetradynamous

Plants having six stamens, two of which are shorter than the others.

Tetrastichous

Flowers or leaves on a stalk arranged in four vertical rows.

Texture

An element of design: the physical, tangible surface of plant material as perceived by the sense of touch (tactile) or sight (visual).

Describes quality such as shiny/dull, silky/rough with colours and lighting influencing the effect of textures. Shiny textures have greater eye-pull. Dull and smooth textures appear to recede.

Thanksgiving Day

An annual day's holiday in the USA, first celebrated by the Pilgrim Fathers at Plymouth in 1621. After the War of Independence its observance became general and from 1863 was annually recommended by the President. In 1941 it was fixed for the fourth Thursday in November as a Thanksgiving to God.

Theme

A unifying idea or topic; expanded into an interpretative exhibit or composition within certain parameters dictated by a show schedule.
See also *Interpretation, Interpretive*

Thinning

The removal of small seedlings from rows or beds, or removing fruit from bushes or trees, in both instances to promote larger growth.

Thorn

A sharp pointed woody extension of a stem.

Thorn stripper

A galvanized spring metal tool with claw-like ends for stripping thorns from stems, especially of roses.

Three-dimensional (or 3D)

Covers height, width and depth, the form in which sculptors work, unlike painters who create sensations of the third dimension on a plane of two dimensions. The form created by three dimensions can either be solid or volumetric.

Tiara head-dress

An elegant style of design for a bride usually made up with one kind of flower.

Tiliaceae   K4-5 or (4-5) C4-5
A∞G̲(2-5)
The Tilia (Lime) is the important

member of this family so far as flower arrangers are concerned.

Tilth

The surface texture of the soil when worked and prior to seed sowing or transplanting. It is created by careful raking and trampling down newly dug ground. It can be described as rough or fine depending on particle size.

Tissue

Groups of cells having the same function; they may be simple, eg parenchyma; or complex, when several types of cell are grouped together. Tissues may be living or dead.

Tissue culture

The process whereby cells from an organism (meristem) are isolated and grown on a medium under clinical and controlled conditions.

Title card

An appropriate and pithy description of the theme or interpretation; a replica of the class title in either decorative or simple form. It can also be a quotation, book title, part of a poem, hymn, proverb, etc, and may always be used in competitive work since it is not an accessory. A title card should always be neatly executed, unobtrusive and appropriate in style of design, lettering, colour and materials.

Tomentose

With a dense woolly pubescence.

Tomentum

A felt-like covering of downy hairs on leaves and other parts of plants.

Tonality
The overall scheme of colours and tones in an arrangement.

Tone (of colour)
Any spectrum colour neutralized by the addition of grey. Also used to describe the quality of a given colour as modified by the addition of white or black (tints and shades).

Tone down
To moderate or soften a colour.

Tonoplast
The membrane enclosing the vacuole of a plant cell.

Toothed
Any of the various small indentations occurring on the margins of a leaf, or petal and variously described as fine, coarse, minute, round, sharp, etc.

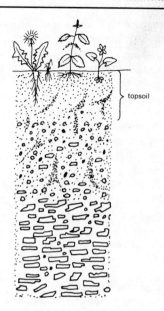

topsoil

Topiary
The art of training and clipping shrubs and trees into intricate shapes and patterns; practised since Roman times.

Topsoil
The uppermost organic layer in a soil profile containing humus and minerals. The feeding roots of most plants are widespread in the topsoil which is more fertile than the subsoil.

Toxin
A poisonous substance produced by some plants to prevent themselves against plant-eating animals (herbivores).

Trace elements
Certain mineral or chemical elements which are essential in very small quantities for good plant growth. They are iron, manganese, boron, copper and zinc.

Tracheid
An elongated, lingified, thin, dead cell with tapering ends in the xylem tissue which acts as a water-conducting cell.

Traditional
Twentieth century style (from Edwardian times to 1939) with clearly stated characteristics such as well defined focal area, stressing orderly radiating growth, massed material with little use of space (but

167

nevertheless including recession). Divided into realistic and decorative categories. Designs were based on geometric forms, triangular, vertical, horizontal, etc. An awareness of colour harmonies, with grouping of colours, and kinds of plant material, with transition in shapes and values are components of a traditional style.

Training

The careful selection and tying up of branches so that they grow in the desired direction for ornamental or utilitarian purposes. Training can be against a wall, over trellis work, arches, posts, pillars and fences.

Transition

The gradual change from one form to another; the grading of plant material is a characteristic of traditional designs. Transition can be a grading of size, shape, line, direction, area, mass or colour value.

Transitional plant material

The various shapes of buds or half-open flowers, the many leaves on stems of foliage and also flowers which are turned from full face in an arrangement, all of which give transition from point material to line material. It is a necessary facet of traditional designs, less important in modern and does not feature in Abstract work.

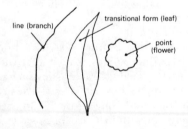

line (branch) transitional form (leaf) point (flower)

Translocation

The movement of substances (mineral and chemical) in the vascular system from one part of a plant to another. There are two main processes:
(1) the uptake of soluble minerals in the xylem from the soil
(2) the transfer of organic compounds, synthesized by leaves, to various growing points within the phloem.

Translucent

Semi-transparent, allowing light to pass through, partially or in a diffused manner.

Transpiration

The loss of water (evaporation) from plants through the stomata of the leaves. Factors affecting the rate of transpiration are light, temperature, wind and humidity. Compare with *Respiration*.

Transplanting

Moving plants from one position to another either to give more space for growing (such as for wallflowers) or, as for trees and shrubs, to keep their root system compact.

Transverse section

A cut across an organ or tissue made at right angles to the main direction of growth, in order to study structure. Abbreviated to TS.
See also *Longitudinal section*

Tree

Any large perennial woody plant with a distinct trunk (normally single) giving rise to an elevated system of branches, leaves and sometimes flowers.

Treillage
Trellis work or lattice craft for supporting climbing plants. Often elaborate constructions in wood and iron.

Triadic colour
A harmony made up of three colours at equal distances on the colour circle (every fourth segment). A contrasting harmony of three hues.

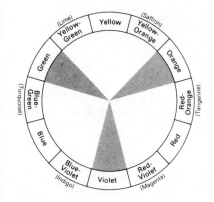

Tribe
A group of related genera within a family, eg Compositae has 13 tribes.

Tribute
Floral tribute or funeral design as a statement of admiration or friendship towards someone.

Trifid
Part pinholder, part floral foam holder, for use where the pinholder supports hollow stemmed flowers and a block of floral foam supports other flowers and foliage.

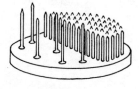

Trifoliate
Having three leaves, leaflike parts, or three leaflets in a compound leaf.

Trivet
A three-legged stand, usually made of metal, which can be a base or support for a flower arrangement or an accessory for a period piece.

Trompe-l'oeil
'Deception of the eye'; the optical illusion of paintings on a wall at the end of an allée giving the impression of additional distance. Also painting on a blind wall to expand the vista.

Tropism
The movement of a plant in response to an external stimulus such as gravity (geotropism) or light (phototropism).

Truncate
Leaf base ending abruptly, as if cut straight across.

Trunk
The main woody stem of a tree, comprising bark, sapwood and heartwood

Truss
A loose cluster of flowers at the end of a stem.

Tube
The lower fused part of a corolla or perianth with united segments.

Tuber
A thick swollen underground stem in which food is stored; it has buds in modified leaf axils from which new plants can grow, eg Dahlia.

Tuberous
A root with parts resembling a tuber or tubers.

Tufa
Soft porous rock consisting of calcium carbonate deposited from springs rich in lime. It is used for rock or alpine sink gardens and is relatively lightweight.

Tungsten light
An incandescent (light produced by heating a filament to high temperature) light emitted from electric lamp bulbs with a tungsten filament. The colour of the light is on the yellow side and this affects some colours, eg reds become more orange and greens and blues take on a greyish appearance. It also affects colour photography, imparting a yellow cast unless film is filtered or tungsten balanced film is used.

Turbinate
The shape of the shells of certain molluscs, taking the form of an inverted cone.

Turf
A grass sward maintained for ornamental purposes; a section cut from a field or lawn comprising earth containing dense growth of grasses with roots. The use of *natural* turf in exhibition work is acceptable and it need not be in water or water-retaining material.

Turfed seat
A construction of bricks or stone on top of which turf was placed along with fragrant plants and which was a feature of enclosed medieval gardens. An illustration appears in 'The Romaunt of the Rose'.

Turgid
The state of cells which cannot absorb any more water by osmosis since the cell wall is expanded to capacity. Turgidity keeps a plant rigid; a decrease in turgidity leads to the plant wilting.

Turgidity
When the living cells of a plant organ contain as much water as possible so that they are each pressing firmly against their cell walls, imparting rigidity to the organ as a whole.

Turntable
(1) A metal stand on which a flat circular top is placed and which then revolves. It is used by floral art demonstrators in order that the arrangement can periodically be turned to the audience to show the construction in progress.

(2) In National shows some classes are occasionally exhibited on turntables which feature motion for a modern exhibit.

Type
The specimen of the individual plant from which a species was first described and accepted for botanical classification or in a more general sense the typical form in cultivation.

U

Umbel
A type of racemose inflorescence in which all the single stalked flowers are the same length and arise from the same point on the flower axis. A compound umbel is an arrangement of several umbels on one stem.

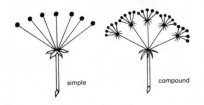

simple   compound

Umbellate
Flowers (inflorescences) in umbels.

Umbelliferae K5 C5 or o A5 Ḡ(2)
A family which includes Eryngium, Astrantia, Ferula (Fennel), Angelica and Sweet Cicely (Myrrhis odorata). Bupleurum is a shrubby member.

Underwiring
The use of wires that are too thin or insufficient to support the plant material, causing it to be uncontrollable. See also *Overwiring*

Undulate
A leaf shape with wavy margins that

are not pronounced enough to be called teeth or lobes.

Unguiculate
Petals contracted at the base like a claw.

Unguis
The claw-like base of certain petals.

Unilocular
Having a single compartment in the ovary. See also *Locule*

Unisexual
A flower which has either male or female organs but not both.

Unit
Two or more items (supported by wires or not, as the case may be) and mounted together prior to assembly into a larger design for a bouquet, etc. See also *Branching unit*, *Natural unit* and *Ribbed unit*

172

Unity
The quality of forming a whole from separate and component parts.

Urceolate
Shaped like an urn or pitcher; an urceolate corolla is wider in the middle than above or below.

V

Vacuole
The liquid-filled space in a cell consisting of water, dissolving sugars and minerals enabling the cell to stay alive.

The outward pressure of the vacuole on the cell wall helps to keep the plant turgid (rigid) when osmosis takes place.

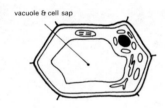

vacuole & cell sap

Valentine
See *St Valentine's Day*

Valerianaceae
Rudimentary C(5) A1-4 G(1-3) Small family which includes Valeriana (Valerian) and Centranthus.

Value   (of colour)
The degree of lightness or darkness of a colour.

Valve
Any of the several parts that make up a dry dehiscent fruit; the sections of a capsule which separate to allow the seeds to escape.

Variation
The use of different types of plant material in a design and can apply to sizes, shapes, colours, textures, etc. Variation gives counter movement which helps to reinforce the main visual movement in a design.

Variegated
Leaves and flowers with two or more colours arising from the absence of chlorophyll in part of the leaf. Variegated plants are very decorative but can only be propagated vegetatively to maintain variegation. Any stems that have reverted must be pruned out of a plant.

Variety
A variant of the species which has small heritable differences from the type. Compare with *cultivar*.

Varnishing
The sealing of wood with a shellac which can be transparent or slightly coloured. Wood and stems can be stained before varnishing if a different colour is required.

Varnishing is 'artificially coloured plant material' in competitive work.

Vascular bundle
The thin strand of vascular tissue containing primary xylem and primary phloem. Many vascular bundles form a vascular cylinder.

They may be found in a leaf or a stem, either scattered (in the case of Mono-cotyledons) or in rings (in non-woody Dicotyledons).

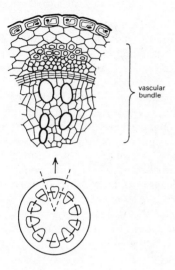

vascular bundle

Vascular tissue
Xylem and phloem; xylem trans-locates water and nutrients from the roots to the stems and leaves. Phloem translocates products of synthesis to other parts of the plant.

Vase
A vessel used either as an ornament or for holding cut flowers. In flower arranging the word has been super-seded by 'container' but it is still used extensively in show schedules and defined as 'a vessel whose height is greater than its width'. See also *Bowl*

Vase counterweight
A construction of a metal strip fashioned into a hook, the other end of which is attached to a lead weight. It is used to balance the back of a large arrangement and prevent it toppling over.

Vegetative
Any part of a plant which is not involved in *sexual* reproduction. Stems, roots and leaves are vegetative organs, flowers are not.

Vegetative propagation
Means of increasing plant stock which thereby ensures the reproduc-tion of indentical characteristics of the parent plant. Vegetative pro-pagation may be carried out by means of stem or root cuttings, division, layering, etc, or by producing an entirely new plant from one organ, eg rhizome, bulb, tuber. See also *Asexual reproduction*

Velutinous
Covered with short dense soft hairs.

Venation
The arrangement of veins in a leaf.

Verbenaceae   K(5) C(5) A4 G̲(2)
Small family of whose herbaceous members Verbena is the most well known. Callicarpa, Caryopteris and Clerodendron are shrubby members.

Vermiculite
Lightweight natural substance (allied to mica) containing magnes-ium and potassium and capable of absorbing large quantities of water. Used for seed germination and root-ing stem cuttings.

Vernalization
The treatment of seeds or bulbs by subjecting them to a particular range of temperature and causing them to move more quickly from a vegetative to a reproductive phase.

Verrucose
Covered with wart-like or nodular growths.

Vertical line
A narow design, relatively tall to other designs and with dominant upward visual movement. The design may be in a tall and narrow container in order to emphasize the vertical line, although not every component needs to point upwards.

Verticil
A circular arrangement of parts of a plant around an axis, eg leaves around a stem. See also *Whorl*

Verticillate
Arranged in whorls or verticils. See also *Verticil*

Vessel
A long water-conducting tube of Xylem having walls thickened by lignin; takes various forms, eg spiral, scalariform (ladder-like ridges), etc.

Viable
The capacity to carry out a function; such as for seeds to be able to germinate when conditions become favourable.

Victorian posy
Traditional form of the posy, comprising concentric rings of small flowers placed around a central (usually rose) bud.

Each ring should be of one colour only, repeated when other colours have been used. It is a polychromatic design suitable for child bridesmaids or, occasionally, by adults. It is finished off with a frill or edged with leaves and can be adorned with ribbon loops. The Victorian posy can be either of natural stems, eventually to stand in a vase, or wired for wedding work.

Villous
Parts of plants bearing long and soft hairs.

Violaceae   K5 C5 A5 G(3)
A family solely of the genus Viola.

Violet
A secondary colour from the mixture of blue and red pigments;
effect under tungsten light: greys slightly

effect under white fluorescent light: intensifies

Opt app	Psycho eff	Symb interp
dark	reserved	spiritual
heavy	quiet	exclusive
deep	soothing	mystery
sombre	absorbing	illusion
mystical	contemplating	fantasy
restrained	serious	martyrdom
richness	melancholy	

Virus

A group of very simple organisms which destroy cells and cause disease which can be transmitted by contact, by insect carrier or grafting diseased material.

Viscid

Cohesive and sticky, such as a leaf or bud covered with sticky substance.

Vista

A view, especially through a long narrow avenue of trees; created in park and garden design from the 17th century onwards.

Visual balance

See *Balance (2)*

Visual weight

The careful use of plant material such that different characteristics are employed to achieve the desired balanced result, eg warm colours carry more 'weight' than cool, rough textures appear heavier than smooth, some closed flower forms have more 'weight' than open forms.

Vittae

Tubelike cavities, containing oil, which occur in the fruits of some Umbelliferae.

Void

An empty space or area between solid elements in a design. Voids should be well-shaped and variation in their sizes is necessary for contrast and interest. No one void should be so wide as to seem visually to split the design.

Volumetric form

Created by the three dimensions of height, width and depth but containing space within, ie opposite to solid form. The form consists of many planes.

W

WAFAS
World Association of Flower Arrangers formed in 1981. The first World Show was held in Bath (UK) in June 1984, the second in Brussels (Belgium) in June 1987. The country responsible for administration changes every three years.

Walled garden
Originated in Persia and Egypt. Developed by the Romans and re-created in medieval times. Adjacent to the house, or an extension of it, the walled garden eventually became a separate feature from the 18th century onwards. Generally the kitchen garden was walled but it may have also included an area for cultivating flowers for the house.

'Warm' colours
See *Colour temperature*

Water-retaining material
A synthetic substance, sometimes called floral foam which absorbs many times its own weight of water and used for staging fresh plant material. Earth, sand and peat are alternative substances and moss, fruit and vegetables can be considered as water retaining material in competitive work, as appropriate.
See also *Floral foam*

Water table
The upper surface of the water-saturated part of the ground which may be from a few centimetres below in soils by rivers, to a metre or more down, according to the area. The water table is not constant and is obviously closer to the surface in winter after considerable rainfall.

Wavy
The margin of a leaf, crinkled or folded in the vertical plane; whereas undulating is curving only on the horizontal plane.

Wedding anniversary
Names are given to many wedding anniversaries in order to indicate the nature of suitable gifts for the occasion. Only the most significant are usually so marked and they are traditional ones, viz
1st Paper
2nd Cotton
3rd Leather

5th	Wood
7th	Woollen
10th	Tin
12th	Silk/fine linen
15th	Crystal
20th	China
25th	Silver
30th	Pearl
40th	Ruby
50th	Golden
60th	Diamond

Weeping

The habit of pendulous branches of trees which often touch the ground. Applies to Weeping Willow, (Salix alba 'Tristis'), some standard roses and Weeping Pear (Pyrus salicifolia 'Pendula').

Well-head

An ornamental garden feature, either directly above a well, in use, or a sham. A wrought-iron crane can likewise be utilitarian or purely ornamental.

Well holder

A heavy metal cylindrical container in the base of which a series of brass pins is set closely together. A well holder holds water and is used either as a small container, or inserted into another container, such as a vase, which by itself is not watertight.

In addition to the metal types there are plastic ones with sloping sides where the pin-holder is detachable or not.

White

An achromatic colour (ie devoid of chroma) of maximum lightness. Ostwald claimed that white should be accepted as a colour, because it is as important as that of the chromatic hues.

White is the complement of Black, the other extreme of the neutral grey series.

Zodiac: Cancer

> *Heraldry:* Argent (silver). Faith and Purity
>
> *effect under tungsten light:* slightly yellow
>
> *effect under white fluorescent light:* white

Opt app	Psycho eff	Symb interp
bright	festive	truth
radiant	peaceful	purity
spacious	brightening	innocence
pure	unemotional	spirituality
light		surrender
cold		hope
		bride (weddings)
		death (historical and mythical)
		honesty
		chastity
		Moon

Whorl

A group of three or more organs, of the same kind, at the same point and arranged in a circle.

Wild flowers
Flora of the British Isles which grow uncultivated out of doors. Some species are protected by conservation laws.

Wild garden
Although part of the scene since gardens were first made, the greatest development came in the 19th century pioneered by William Robinson and Gertrude Jekyll. A greater awareness of wild gardening is now being fostered and several books on the subject have been published recently.

Wilt
Lack of water within plants causes loss of cell turgidity and leaves droop. Also a condition caused by disease or toxins.

Windbreak
A hedge, fence, or wall which lessens the force of strong prevailing winds and serves as a protection to plants. See also *Shelter-belt*

Window-box
A long narrow box, affixed to a window sill, in which plants are grown. Can be re-planted for different seasons or established with hardy evergreens and trailing plants. In town houses and flats it affords the only means of growing flowering and foliage plants outside.
See also *Window-gardening*

Window-gardening
A common practice in Victorian times before Nathanial Ward invented his 'case'. Ranged from a few pots on the window sill indoors to more elaborate and complicated

180

arrangements of troughs, trellis work and even fountains.

Winged
With one or more thin, flat projections or flanges, eg winged seed of Sycamore. See also *Samara*

Wire
Flexible metal finely drawn into various thicknesses for wiring down flowers and foliage for support. Packaged in bundles of various thicknesses and lengths.

Wire is either Black, Blue annealed, or Silver. Some thicknesses are also available on reels. Wire covered in green plastic is also available for tying ribbon.

Lengths   7 in. = 180 mm
           10 in. = 260 mm
           12 in. = 310 mm
           14 in. = 360 mm

Thicknesses

SWG	Metric equivalent
18	1.25 mm
19	1.00 mm
20	0.90 mm
22	0.70 mm
24	0.56 mm
26	0.46 mm
28	0.38 mm
30	0.32 mm
32	0.28 mm
34	0.24 mm
36	0.20 mm

Wire-mesh (netting)
See *Chicken-wire*

Wiring

Several methods of supporting, anchoring and controlling flowers, stems and foliage by the use of wire in various thicknesses and different techniques.

Wiring is permitted in competitive Floral Art if well executed and inconspicuous. The cut stems of fresh plant material must be in water or water-retaining material, wired or not. See also *Internal wiring*

Wood

The hard structural and water-conducting tissue composed of secondary xylem and other cells found in trees and shrubs.

Wounding

The removal of a sliver of cork cambium of a woody stem cutting in order to induce quicker rooting.

Wrack

Common name for a number of brown algae of the Fucus species which includes the seaweeds.

Wreath

An adaptation of the garlands of flowers placed on tombs and statues as tokens of memory. Historically it can also be a circular ornament of ribbons, flowers or leaves for victors or conquerors especially in Greek and Roman times. The circular wreath of today is to honour and commemorate the departed and is a symbol of eternal life.

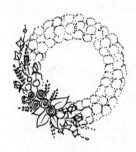

X

Xeromorphic
Plants or parts of plants which have characteristics serving as protection against excessive loss of water.

Xerophyte
A plant adapted to survive long periods without moisture, eg cacti and succulents.

Xylem
Tissue in the vascular system in both roots and stems allowing water and nutrients to enter at roots, up the stems and to the leaves. Most are dead cells with lignin strengthening tissue.

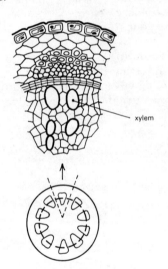

xylem

Y

Yellow

Primary colour, centre of highest luminosity of the spectrum with the highest reflection and transmission values. One of the most favoured of all colours and associated with the sun and light.

Zodiac: Leo

Heraldry: Or (Gold). Honour and Loyalty

effect under tungsten light: vivid orange-yellow

effect under white fluorescent light: strong greenish-yellow

Opt app	Psycho eff	Symb interp
bright	uplifting	Springtime
light	stimulating	cheerfulness
open	relaxing	cowardice
radiant	evoking	deceit
luminous	expectation	envy
lively	illuminating	jealousy
advancing		sublimity
clean		inspiration
expansive		optimism
		disease
		(sickness)
		message

Yellow/green (Lime/spring-green)

A tertiary colour obtained from the mixture of yellow and green pigments.

Zodiac: Libra   *Heraldry:* not used

effect under tungsten light: yellowish green

effect under white fluorescent light: slightly brightened

Opt app	Psycho eff	Symb interp
light	restful	youth
clear	meek	kindness
pure		
soft		

Yellow/orange (saffron)

A tertiary colour obtained from the mixture of yellow and orange pigments.

Opt app	Psycho eff	Symb interp
radiant	warming	sunshine
warm	exhilarating	wealth
bright	inducing	mirth
shining	happiness	happiness
sunny		fertility
striking		sun
expansive		

Z

Zone of differentiation

The area further back from the apex of a root where the cells are elongated, the outermost layer of which produces the root hairs. These hairs increase the surface area of a root and assist in the uptake of water and nutrients.

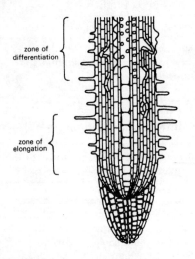

Zygomorphic

Flowers which are bilaterally symmetrical, ie giving a mirror image when cut along one plane only.
See also *Actinomorphic*

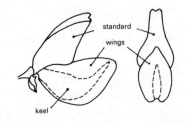

Zygote

A cell formed by the union of two gametes. A fertilized ovum is a zygote.

Zone of elongation

Behind the meristem of a root is a smooth section where individual cells undergo changes and become elongated.

Classification of the Plant Kingdom

chart overleaf

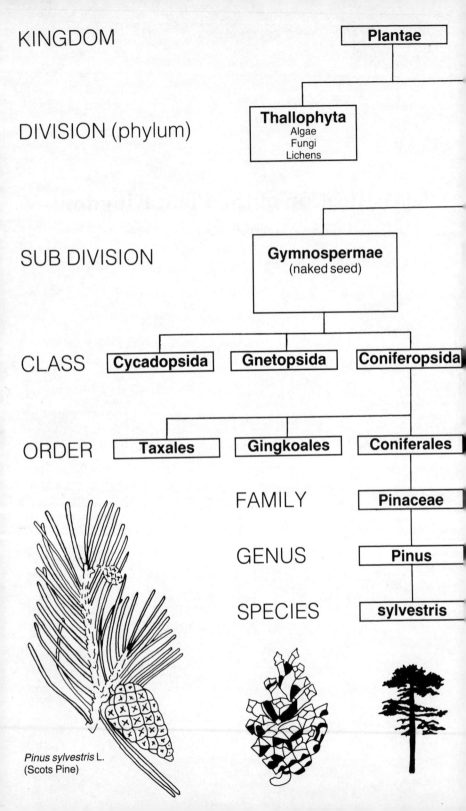

KINGDOM	**Plantae**
DIVISION (phylum)	**Thallophyta** Algae Fungi Lichens
SUB DIVISION	**Gymnospermae** (naked seed)
CLASS	**Cycadopsida** · **Gnetopsida** · **Coniferopsida**
ORDER	**Taxales** · **Gingkoales** · **Coniferales**
FAMILY	**Pinaceae**
GENUS	**Pinus**
SPECIES	**sylvestris**

Pinus sylvestris L.
(Scots Pine)

Classification

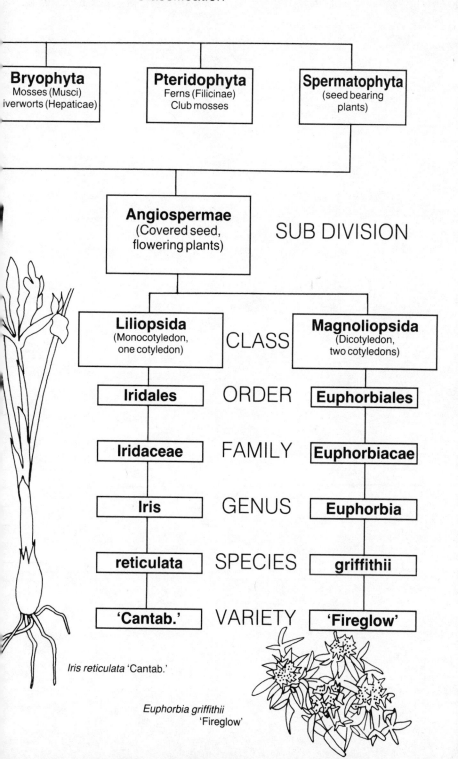

Bryophyta
Mosses (Musci)
iverworts (Hepaticae)

Pteridophyta
Ferns (Filicinae)
Club mosses

Spermatophyta
(seed bearing
plants)

Angiospermae
(Covered seed,
flowering plants)

SUB DIVISION

Liliopsida
(Monocotyledon,
one cotyledon)

CLASS

Magnoliopsida
(Dicotyledon,
two cotyledons)

Iridales   ORDER   **Euphorbiales**

Iridaceae   FAMILY   **Euphorbiacae**

Iris   GENUS   **Euphorbia**

reticulata   SPECIES   **griffithii**

'Cantab.'   VARIETY   **'Fireglow'**

Iris reticulata 'Cantab.'

Euphorbia griffithii
'Fireglow'